Dollmakers

AND THEIR STORIES

Dollmakers

AND THEIR STORIES

Women Who Changed
the World of Play

~ *Krystyna Poray Goddu* ~

Henry Holt and Company

NEW YORK

Henry Holt and Company, LLC
Publishers since 1866
115 West 18th Street
New York, New York 10011
www.henryholt.com

Henry Holt is a registered trademark of Henry Holt and Company, LLC

Library of Congress Cataloging-in-Publication Data
Goddu, Krystyna Poray.
    Dollmakers and their stories : women who changed the world of
play / Krystyna Poray Goddu.—1st ed.
         p.   cm.
    Summary: Profiles five of the women behind the most important
dolls of the past century, and introduces six women making dolls
today.
    Includes bibliographical references.
    Contents: Martha Chase: 1851–1925 — Käthe Kruse: 1883–1968 —
Sasha Morgenthaler: 1893–1975 — Beatrice Alexander Behrman:
1895–1990 — Ruth Handler: 1916–2002 — Today's women and the
future of dolls.
    ISBN-13: 978-0-8050-7257-0
    ISBN-10: 0-8050-7257-8
    1. Dollmakers—United States—Biography. 2. Dolls—United
States—History—20th century. [1. Dollmakers. 2. Dolls—History—
20th century. 3. Women—Biography.]   I. Title.
NK4894.15G63 2004
745.592'21'092273—dc22
    [B]   2003063961

First edition—2004 / Designed by Meredith Pratt
Printed in the United States of America on acid-free paper. ∞
   10 9 8 7 6 5 4 3 2 1

For Anna and Jack,
whose creative spirits are always an inspiration

Author's Note

Your great-great-grandmother probably played with homemade rag dolls that are worlds removed from today's realistic babies that eat, wet, and talk back. Your vinyl fashion dolls, be they Barbies or Bratz, echo nineteenth-century fashionable porcelain ladies in concept only. And even fifty years ago, no one would have dreamed that chubby creatures with squished-in faces, claiming to come from the Cabbage Patch, would win a place in children's hearts.

As dramatically as these playthings have changed over the centuries, however, the strong bond between girls and their dolls has remained constant. Whether you enjoy playing with your dolls or displaying them, you are part of a long tradition. For some girls, dolls are a passing childhood fancy. But for many others, fondness for these treasured companions never fades. A childhood love of dolls can inspire a rich and rewarding adult passion. Collecting dolls—whether antiques or contemporary creations—can be a mature expression of the same instinct that first draws a child to play. Working with dolls—

either as an artist or as a businesswoman or, as many women do, as both—can be a deeply rewarding endeavor.

In this book you'll meet the women behind some of the most important dolls of the past hundred years. They each understood that no matter how the world changes, children will always need to play with dolls. In the turbulent world of the late 1960s, Madame Alexander said: "What a doll does for a little girl is develop her capacity to love others and herself." Decades earlier, in Germany, Käthe Kruse wrote that her mission was to create "a child for the child." Contemporary designer Robin Woods found her way to a career in dollmaking by witnessing troubled children's lack of a "play life." These women's visions of what a doll should—or could—be have made it possible for some of your favorite dolls to come into being. May their stories inspire your own creative spirit.

Contents

Today's Women and the Future of Dolls

Dollmakers

AND THEIR STORIES

Introduction

Girls have played with dolls since ancient times. From the simplest stick and clay figures to today's interactive playthings, toys made in the human likeness have always been an integral part of girlhood. The way children play with dolls has not changed much over the centuries. But the dolls themselves have changed dramatically. And although the new ideas, new designs, and new technologies of many men have transformed dolls, some of the most important changes have been made by women.

For centuries, dolls were most often made at home, fashioned from readily available materials: wood, cloth, leather, even dried apples or corn husks. But as early as the fourteenth century, wealthy families were able to buy dolls for their children to play with, and these were made to represent adults in elaborate clothing. For just as children were dressed as miniature adults until the middle of the eighteenth century, so, too, were dolls. Not until the mid-1700s do we begin to see what we think of as baby dolls, and even then there were not many of them until the mid-1800s.

The first recorded makers of dolls were a pair named Otto and Mess, who registered themselves in Germany in 1465. We know nothing about what kinds of dolls they made, but because drawings and prints dating from the late 1400s show men carving and jointing wooden dolls, we can assume that from about that time on, jointed wooden dolls were being made for sale — by men.

By the middle of the nineteenth century, commercial doll manufacturers were producing precious and beautiful dolls from china, wax, and porcelain. Stylishly dressed in shiny silk gowns and smooth velvet cloaks, with long, soft human-hair locks and luminous glass eyes, these dolls were coveted by girls everywhere but owned only by the very fortunate. Even then, they were often meant to be displayed — at a tea table, on a dresser, in a carriage — or played with very carefully, for they were both heavy and fragile. The factories that made them were owned by businessmen like Emile Jumeau and Casimir Bru in France and Armand Marseille and Kammer & Reinhardt in Germany. There were occasional women who were successful dollmakers, such as Madame Huret, who created some of the most beautiful fashion dolls in France, and Augusta Montanari and Lucy Peck, who both made wax dolls in England. But generally, it was men who ruled the business of dolls and so dictated the manner of girls' play in the nineteenth century. Men continued to determine what kinds of dolls were made and sold in the twentieth century as doll companies sprang up and flourished in the United States.

At home, however, it was the mothers who ruled over playtime. In many households, it was the mothers, or other female relatives, who made dolls for their daughters' play. They made them from the materials in their workbaskets, usually cloth and wool, often left over from making their own clothing or household items. It was the mothers, too, who watched their children play, even in wealthy families. Observant mothers noted the kinds of games young imaginations dreamed up and which dolls were the favorites. And so it seems only natural that as time went on, it was the mothers who began to change the way commercial dolls were made.

Our story begins, then, with women—most of them mothers—who rebelled against the precious dolls produced by men and looked to make dolls that would truly appeal to girls of all economic classes, dolls for hearty play as well as tender care. They were women like the American entrepreneur Martha Chase, whose cloth dolls, first made as "amusements" for herself and neighborhood children, led to a successful cottage industry, and the unconventional German Käthe Kruse, whose husband told her to "make your own" when she asked him to buy their daughters some dolls. Her first creation led to award-winning cloth dolls and a company that thrives today. There was the Swiss artist Sasha Morgenthaler, whose unrelenting need to create an aesthetic durable plaything forged a path to the popular Sasha doll, and the feisty Beatrice Alexander, daughter of Eastern European immigrants, who began making dolls on New York City's Lower East Side and started what continues to be one of the best-known American doll companies in the world. And while most girls don't know who Ruth Handler is, almost every girl can recognize her brainchild, Barbie, which revolutionized the possibilities of the fashion doll.

These were creative women with vision, ambition, and determination. Each of them pushed the boundaries of a woman's role in her era to bring a new genre of doll to children around the world. Strong feminists of their day, they competed in male worlds and won on their own terms. In pursuing their visions, they defied the social mores of their times. Their resulting creations became an intrinsic part of childhood for generations of girls.

These pioneering women lived in different times, some in different countries. They came from different backgrounds. But they all, at some time in their lives, found that their imaginations had been taken over by the dolls they needed to create. Each one of them overcame obstacles of technical challenge, money, prejudice, and personal despair to fulfill her creative urge. Each of these women's accomplishments prepared the way for the next step to be taken years later by another. The stories of their inspiration are deeply personal. The ways each woman achieved success, however, present a larger panorama of the changing artistic and business environments of the twentieth century, as well as of the evolution of women's roles.

Girls today are encouraged to find examples of women to emulate in nearly every field of endeavor: business, science, technology, and the arts. Much is made of the notion that in earlier times women could not step beyond the prescribed boundaries for success: mothering, teaching, nursing. Yet throughout time, in every field, from Elizabeth Blackwell, doctor, to Maria Mitchell, astronomer, to Louisa May Alcott, writer, to Mary Cassatt, painter, there have been women who defied these standards. These women remain well known. Among them, standing in their shadows but every bit as brave, creative, and pioneering, are the dollmakers, women like Martha Chase, Käthe Kruse, Sasha Morgenthaler, Beatrice Alexander, and Ruth Handler. Following in their footsteps are contemporary women like Pleasant Rowland, Helen Kish, Martha Armstrong-Hand, Robin Woods, Yue-Sai Kan, and Lorna Miller Sands. It is time for these women's stories to be told. We can learn much about toys, dolls, and business and much about art and creativity from them. But we can also learn what many of us want to know most: we can learn what it takes to make our dreams come true.

Martha Chase

(1851–1925)

In the middle of the nineteenth century, when Martha Jenks Wheaton was a young girl, most American girls entertained themselves with handiwork. Publications such as the *American Girl's Book* and *The American Girls Handy Book: How to Amuse Yourself and Others* encouraged making things and provided patterns and directions. The *American Girl's Book*'s precise instructions for making "a common linen doll" mention at the end that "some little girls make a dozen of these dolls together and play at school with them." Wealthy girls might be fortunate enough to own fragile French porcelain dolls with glass eyes, mohair wigs, and silk clothing, but *The American Girls Handy Book* advises even those girls that when summer comes, they should "leave the city doll in her city home, safe out of harm's way, and manufacture, from materials

to be found in the country, one more suited to country surroundings." Instructions for making dolls from corn husks,
corncobs, and common garden flowers, like petunias and
daisies, follow this advice.

Most girls in the 1850s and 1860s were happy to have as
companions cloth dolls made by a mother's, grandmother's, or
older sister's hand. Rag dolls made from linen or unbleached
cotton stuffed with bran, sawdust, or straw were a popular
Christmas present. Usually they had flat faces with embroi-
dered or painted features. In her autobiographical novel, *Little
House in the Big Woods*, about growing up in Wisconsin in the
1860s, Laura Ingalls Wilder describes her treasured Christmas gift, Charlotte: "She was a beautiful doll. She had a face of
white cloth with black button eyes. A black pencil had made
her eyebrows, and her cheeks and mouth were red with the
ink made from pokeberries. Her hair was black yarn that had
been knit and raveled, so that it was curly. She had little flan-
nel stockings and little black cloth gaiters for shoes, and her
dress was pretty pink and blue calico."

While Laura Ingalls Wilder was growing up in the Wis-
consin woods, Martha Jenks Wheaton was growing up in
Pawtucket, Rhode Island, just outside the state capital of
Providence. She was born on February 12, 1851, into a promi-
nent family. In fact, her ancestor Josef Jenks Jr. had founded
Pawtucket, and her family had been instrumental in the
growth of the community since that time. Her father, James
Wheaton, was a well-known doctor in town, and her mother,

Anna Marie Wheaton, worked tirelessly on projects to benefit the community and was one of the founders of the Homeopathic Hospital in Providence.

Like all little girls of her era, Martha was taught to sew, embroider, and practice the domestic arts. But her own favorite cloth doll had a special pedigree: it was a simple but beautiful creation by one of America's first dollmakers, another Rhode Island native, Izannah Walker. It is rumored that Martha's father was Izannah Walker's doctor, and that is how she obtained one of these oil-painted cloth dolls with molded features. Whether or not this is true, Martha was lucky to have played with such a fine example of the earliest American cloth doll to be patented.

Martha was only a teenager when she married Dr. William L. White and a widow before the age of twenty, for her first husband

Shown here as a teenager in the 1860s, Martha Chase, the daughter of a well-known Rhode Island physician, grew up in a prominent Rhode Island family.

died in 1870. Before too many years had passed, however, she fell in love with another doctor, Julian Chase, a graduate of Harvard Medical School who was training in her father's office. She and Julian wedded in April 1873, and over the next three years Martha gave birth to two daughters, Bessie and Anna.

With toddler and infant in tow, the couple sailed from Boston for Europe on September 30, 1876, where Julian was to complete his medical training in Vienna, Austria. Martha, who had an organized and efficient nature, practiced the European style of housekeeping on a budget in four small rooms. Keeping up the domestic skills she had learned as a young girl was second nature; Martha sewed the children's clothing, pillowcases, sheets, and table linens.

Toys were plentiful in Vienna, and gifts arrived from home, too, but the deep-seated habit of handiwork prevailed for their first Christmas abroad. "I have made a doll for Bessie for a Christmas present," she wrote in the detailed journal she kept during the years abroad, "just such a one as old Dinah at home, only not as large. The face and hands are knit from black woolen yarn, and the stockings are from red yarn. It is dressed in green trimmed with a feather stitching of red yarn for a skirt and a red waist and white apron, collar and cuffs. The wool for the hair is made of black yarn wound round my finger and tied, and then sewed onto the head." Though Martha did not find any special pleasure in creating the doll,

Bessie loved it, Martha wrote later. "The kitty and the black dolly are her favorites," she noted.

During the years in Europe, Martha watched her girls play with their dolls. One day she wrote in her journal: "Bessie played all day long by herself and talks to her playthings as though they were alive. She sees a dolly in everything, a stick of wood, a rag, a piece of paper, a bootjack, anything she can carry around has to be treated as though it were a baby." A few months later, when Anna was a bit older, the girls could play together, she noted with some delight: "They play very prettily together all sorts of things, but their favorite play is to each take a doll and walk side by side round and round the table, talking to each other. Generally, Bessie says she is going to the sugar baker's to buy sugar for the dolly."

By the early 1880s, the family had settled back in Rhode Island, and before too long, Bessie and Anna were joined by another sister and two brothers. (Martha bore seven children, but the two other boys, twins, died when they were babies.) The 1880s were filled with caring for her children and her husband and, in her family tradition, community involvement. While keeping up with her household and civic duties, Martha continued making cloth dolls for her children and eventually for other neighborhood children as well. "I first made the dolls . . . as an amusement and to see what I could do," Martha wrote in a 1917 letter quoted in the magazine *Toys and Novelties*. "For several years I did this, and gave the dolls away to the neighborhood children. Then, by chance, a store buyer saw one and insisted upon my taking an order." The "chance" Martha refers to occurred in 1891, when she took one of her dolls to Jordan Marsh, a large department store in Boston, in search of a pair of shoes for it. The buyer for the store's toy department saw the doll and asked where Martha had bought it. When Martha left Jordan Marsh that day, she had shoes for her doll. She also had an order to make dolls for the prestigious store.

Back home, Martha consulted with her family. All agreed that she should accept the order, and so Martha officially started her dollmaking company. She first installed the business in a small building behind her home at 22 Park Place in Pawtucket but soon took over Julian's garage. Finally Julian built her a workshop of her own, which became known as the Dolls' House and the official home of the M. J. Chase Company.

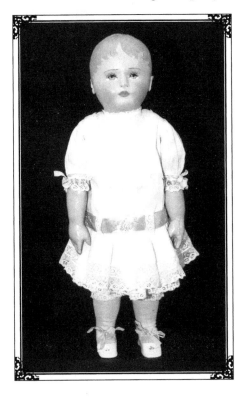

This seventeen-inch doll is dressed just as she would have looked when she came from the Chase factory.

Martha used a material known as stockinet—a soft, elastic cotton similar to that used for socks and stockings at the time—for her dolls' heads and a heavy white cotton for the bodies. These soft and sturdy materials made her dolls radically different both from the heavy yet fragile bisque of the still-popular German and French dolls and from the floppier raglike homemade dolls less-wealthy children owned.

Martha hired women from town to work with her both in the Dolls' House and in their own homes. The women who worked at home, known as outworkers, sewed and stuffed the dolls' arms, legs, and bodies, and made the clothing. All the dolls' parts came back to the workshop in Martha's backyard, where they were assembled by the women who worked there. Martha oversaw the finishing of every doll at the same time as she and two other women, who sat on a raised dais at one end of the large workroom, painted the dolls' faces and hair.

A booklet issued by the M. J. Chase Company titled *How Chase Dolls Are Made* described the process to potential buyers:

> The manufacture of the Chase Stockinet Doll, from the first stroke of the shears to the last painted eyelash or lock of hair, is fascinating to watch. It is handmade by trained craftsmen of specially wove stockinet, stuffed with clean white cotton batting, till it has the natural lifelike responsive body of a young child. It is painted with the purest and best paint obtainable and completely waterproof so that it may be bathed at will, kept sanitary

and perfectly safe for the child to handle. In fact the child
can take it right into the tub.

The mysterious shapes and forms which the shears cut
out are quickly sewed into arms and legs, with elbows
and knees and fingers and toes. They are then stuffed
with cotton batting till hard and firm as flesh and blood.

The head also is made of stockinet and cotton. But the
remarkable thing is that the delicate features are all so
real and beautiful—raised like the features of a bisque
doll, formed and hardened by a special process so that a
child cannot crush them.

When finally assembled the doll is sent to the studio
where it is thoroughly waterproofed from head to feet
and then painted to look like a real girl or a real boy, with
pink ears, smiling eyes, wavy hair, round cheeks and
pudgy nose.

Although even Izannah Walker in the 1870s had patented her
dollmaking process, Martha Chase never patented hers. Her
method was well known: she stiffened the stockinet with a
gluelike varnish called sizing and then pressed the sized stockinet into plaster molds. She sized it again on the inside and
pressed sized cotton to fill interior areas like the nose and chin.
The origin of her molds, however, was always kept secret.
Many decades later, when the business was sold, German
bisque and composition doll heads were found hidden far
away in the Dolls' House. Some still had bits of plaster on
them—meaning that most likely Martha made the molds for

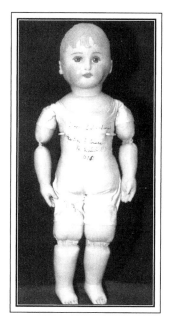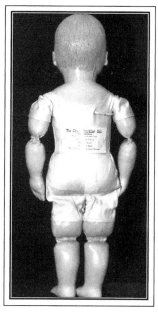

The front of this undressed seventeen-inch doll is signed: "Originated and made by Martha J. Chase, Pawtucket, R.I. 1891." The date probably refers to the start of Martha's factory, for the doll itself dates from approximately 1911. On its back, the doll bears its original label, stating: "The Chase Stockinet Doll. Made of Stockinet and Cloth. Stuffed with Cotton. Made by Hand. Painted by Hand. Made by Especially Trained Workers."

her dolls from doll heads she bought in stores. If this is true, it would answer the question why she never tried to patent her dolls. She knew the head designs were not her originals. Yet her method of using them turned them into completely different dolls.

It is ironic that Martha relied on German doll heads for her original molds, because her dollmaking philosophy was a rebellion against everything the European dolls stood for. She believed that the heavy china and bisque dolls made by the

German and French companies were too heavy for small children's hands and dangerous when they chipped or cracked, which was often. She also, like other mothers of her time, disliked the elaborate dress of the European dolls and worried that because the dolls children played with could not be washed, they carried germs. When she began her own dollmaking company, Martha was determined to create dolls that were soft, safe, and sanitary—opposite in every way from the French and German playthings.

She also ran her business in a very different style than most companies run by men in the late nineteenth and early twentieth centuries. She created a congenial and productive workplace where women worked in respectful collaboration with each other. She hired only women, and they loved to come to work. They were encouraged to feel close to the dolls they made, and one recalled: "When a new member of the doll family appeared, each of us took the one we liked best and had our pictures taken in the yard." Martha also made time for celebrations. For example, "When the 13th of the month came on a Friday, it was, in [Martha Chase's] mind, a 'red-letter day' and she gave us a party saying it was our lucky day!" Martha remembered each woman's birthday and was generous at Easter and at Christmas. Everybody had the month of August off.

The homelike atmosphere of the Dolls' House was strengthened when Martha's daughters, Bessie and Anna, came to work with their mother as well. Artistic Bessie graduated from the Rhode Island School of Design and painted the dolls' faces. She lived at home with her parents, while the more business-minded Anna, married and living next door with her husband, managed the company from across the driveway. Even Martha's sons, Robert and Julian, eventually contributed to the business.

Martha sold her dolls through mail order and in the finest stores of the day, such as FAO Schwarz, Macy's, and Marshall Fields. Her dolls were advertised in important magazines, such as *Vogue* and *Ladies' Home Journal.* The ads emphasized the high quality of the dolls, declaring, for example: "If Stradivarius had made dolls he would have made the Chase Stockinet Doll." In addition to her standard line of children's dolls, in 1905 Martha experimented with a series of character dolls from the Alice in Wonderland stories, a Mammy Nurse and two Pickaninnies from the Uncle Remus stories by Joel Chandler Harris, and a group of figures from Charles Dickens's books. In 1908 she also created a doll representing George Washington. Because these dolls are so difficult to find today, we can guess that she did not make very many and soon returned to concentrating on her play dolls.

In 1910, however, she was presented with a challenge that, with her family's strong medical connections, she could not turn down. Mrs. Lauder Sutherland, principal of the Training School for Nurses at Hartford Hospital in Connecticut, wrote asking if Martha could make an adult-size doll to train nurses in caring for patients. While such a doll was a far cry from the playthings made by the Chase Doll Company, Martha met the challenge. In 1911 she sent the first hospital mannequin, which stood five feet four inches tall but was otherwise constructed exactly like the Chase play dolls, to Hartford Hospital. In 1914 the mannequins, which came to be known as Chase Hospital Dolls—or to the nurses who used them, Mrs. Chase—were exhibited at a nursing convention and became available to hospitals throughout the country. Before Martha's hospital dolls, nurses had practiced caring for patients using straw-filled dummies. The Chase Hospital Dolls were much more realistic and therefore in great demand. Soon after that,

Martha added a baby doll, representing a two-month-old infant, to the hospital line. Nurses could now learn to care for infants on a realistic baby doll as well. Eventually the company was

Made for nurses to practice patient care, this early child Hospital Doll includes realistic features, such as nostrils and ear canals.

making a series of hospital dolls representing children of several ages. Demand for the Chase Hospital Dolls soon exceeded the demand for the playthings, and more and more of the production was devoted to these dolls.

But Martha continued to make play dolls, representing both boys and girls in sizes ranging from twelve to thirty inches. They wore simple school or play clothes and had painted (almost always blond) hair in short styles, some with bangs and bobs, some with side parts and swirls. They ranged in price from $2.40 to $7.50 — not quite as expensive as the European dolls, but far from cheap.

True to her family heritage of community involvement, Martha did not focus only on her business. She promoted education for girls and established domestic studies as part of the curriculum of local schools. She also taught sewing and doll-making in the community. At the Church Hill School, she taught girls to sew doll parts for eight-inch dolls, which were then finished and painted at the Dolls' House and given back to the girls to keep.

Family involvement remained strong and allowed the company to stay securely in family hands after Martha's death in 1925. Anna continued to run the business until her own retirement in 1947, when Martha's grandson, Robert Chase, took over. He emphasized production of the hospital dolls and instigated a new, modern style of play doll, still waterproof but made of vinyl. When he himself retired in 1978, he sold the

Even with the success of her doll company, Martha Chase continued her family heritage of community involvement by promoting education for girls.

company to a medical supply company in Chicago, which stopped making the play dolls altogether. By 1981 the Chase Doll Company had closed.

Long before then, though, the influence of Martha Chase had penetrated deep into the toy industry as like-minded women continued to create dolls meant for a child's hands and imagination. In Europe and in America, the women who followed Martha Chase built on the foundation she laid of integrity in design, production, and entrepreneurship. The popularity of her soft, safe, unadorned dolls and the success of her female-centered business established Martha Chase as a pioneer of feminist thought and activity. One of the earliest American women entrepreneurs, Martha Chase not only created a better plaything for girls, she also created a better workplace for women.

Käthe Kruse

(1883–1968)

*H**ome for lonely Käthe Kruse was a* single gloomy room on a busy city street, which she shared with her seamstress mother. While there was much her mother could not provide for her, she did shower Käthe with love and affection, ensuring that her daughter grew into an open-hearted adult. Käthe's desire to share that love led to the creation of the warm and sturdy cloth dolls that continue to be cherished by children today.

She was born Katharina Simon on September 17, 1883, in the town of Breslau, in southeastern Germany. (Today the town of Breslau is the Polish town of Wroclaw.) Her parents were in love but not married, for her father was already unhappily married to a woman thirteen years older than himself. A civil servant, he lived a typical middle-class life with his family. His discontent, however, eventually led him into romance with Käthe's mother.

Käthe's mother's parents, the Simons, had been farmers, and her mother, one of seventeen children, had lost her parents to illness when she was twelve. Not all of the children survived the difficult life that followed their parents' deaths, and Käthe knew only her aunt Paula, who played an important role in the girl's future. Her hardworking mother, who passed on the qualities of steadfastness and levelheadedness to Käthe as well, became a seamstress. Her skills brought wealthy women of the region to the room that served both as sewing workshop and home for her and her daughter.

In that room, young Käthe would sit in the corner with her schoolbooks while her mother sat at the sewing machine, working with her eyes reddened from fatigue, until all hours of the night. In that room, too, they ate and slept—though far too little. In her autobiography, *Das grosse Puppenspiel* (*The Great Doll Game*), Käthe remembers how she could not fall asleep unless she was holding her mother's hand. Her mother, who must have been torn between the love she wanted to give her child and the need to return to the sewing machine, found a way to coax Käthe to sleep. "She would pull her hand back, very carefully and gently, until I was only holding her finger. Then she would slowly substitute the handle of a cooking spoon for her finger and return to her work." The little girl would sleep, comforted, with her hand wrapped around the wooden handle.

Fridays were a special day for Käthe. On Fridays she spent the afternoon with her father. At midday she would go to the city hall, where he worked, and knock on his window. Her father would soon appear, and the two would do small errands together and take long walks that tired them both. Her father never failed to buy a small amount of groceries for Käthe's mother, whose pride did not allow her to accept anything more from him. Käthe's favorite stop was the cheese store, where she always received a tasty treat. At the end of the afternoon they would return to the gloomy room on Teich Street but "never without a big splendid bouquet of field flowers, which I would pick and tie at my father's instruction," Käthe recalled.

Käthe awaited Fridays with a mixture of dread and excitement. Her father was a moody man, and she never knew which way his mood would swing. Later she came to understand that his unpredictable nature was a result of feeling torn between his two lives: the daily pattern of his middle-class home with his unhappy wife and two sons and the Fridays in the small room on Teich Street with his daughter and her mother.

One of Käthe's mother's customers was the Baroness von Richthofen, and to her delight, Käthe was sometimes invited to spend free days at the von Richthofens' villa outside the city, playing in the gardens with the many animals the family kept. From these visits she developed a deep love for animals, which she never lost. Her fondness for small living creatures was, in fact, far greater than her feeling for any toys or dolls. While she was good to her dolls and used to long for one expensive doll in a fancy shop's store window, no doll of her own ever claimed a special place in her heart. In fact, the opposite occurred. For her eighth birthday, Aunt Paula gave her a doll named Perdita. Käthe described Perdita as a doll with "an hourglass-waisted leather body, dangling legs, and an awful staring stupid doll face. Aunt Paula dressed her in a ladylike purple outfit. She was not alive!" the little girl protested to herself and, after Aunt Paula had left, told her mother, "I cannot love Perdita."

Aunt Paula did not err, however, when, a few years later, she began to take her niece to the theater. Aunt Paula and her husband, Robert, were avid theatergoers and attended plays weekly. Käthe's practical mother did not protest these outings, and Käthe lived for them. She became totally enraptured by the theater, worshiping the talented young actresses of the day and learning roles by heart. By the time Käthe was sixteen, she was determined to become an actress herself, and her mother, though against the idea, could not deny her daughter. Käthe left school and was accepted as an acting student by one of the great actors of the Breslau Municipal Theater.

Her dramatic studies went extremely well, and one year later she was offered an acting job in the bustling city of Berlin. Her salary was to be an impressive 250 marks a month, so without hesitation, she and her mother left for Berlin. It was 1900 and Käthe Kruse was seventeen years old and away from home for the first time. She was amazed by city life—"What a city!" she wrote. "A city pulsating by day and night.... I thought that I would never trust myself to cross the road." She took the stage name Hedda Simon and worked hard. She received good reviews from the critics and toured Europe, giving performances that met with great acclaim. Her talent also quickly brought her attention from the artistic circles of Berlin, which included the sculptor Max Kruse.

Max was a quiet member of this group; he spoke only when he had something to say, and he did not try to promote himself or his works. Thirty years older than Käthe, he had an air of peace and stability that the young woman had never experienced but always longed for. She fell in love with him almost as quickly as he fell in love with her. Within a year, she gave birth to their child, Maria, whom they called Mimerle. Käthe was just nineteen but couldn't have been happier. She saw no need for marriage; love was enough. Having a baby to adore and care for, with Max at her side, seemed to fulfill what she had longed for her entire life. She gave up her acting career and soon was pregnant with a second child. She and Max decided that the busy city of Berlin was no place to bring up children, and so Käthe, with her mother, two small daughters, and a maid, moved to a small cottage near Ascona in southern Switzerland.

Käthe lived peacefully in the countryside, caring for her children, painting, and writing a book for Max, who had encouraged her to develop her artistic side while living away from him. Her life felt simple and harmonious.

It was two-year-old Mimerle who unwittingly changed her mother's life. As she watched her mother tend to her baby sister, christened Sophie but called Finerle or Fifi, she soon requested "a child like yours." As Christmas 1905 approached, Käthe asked Max to find Mimerle a doll in Berlin. Max tried to fulfill the request but was horrified by the lavish porcelain dolls he found in shop after shop. His artistic nature could not tolerate the notion of such a stiff plaything for his daughter. He wrote back to Käthe, indignant, refusing to buy a porcelain doll. How, he asked her, could "such a hard, cold, and stiff object kindle maternal love? Make your own dolls. It's a marvelous chance to develop your artistic skill."

The young mother took his words to heart. She had only the materials at hand in her cottage, so she filled a kitchen towel with sand, knotted parts of it to give the impression of a baby's floppy limbs, and attached a potato for the head. Mimerle was delighted, adoring her soft, warm, and heavy doll because it felt and moved almost like a real baby. The doll had a short life span: the sand began to sift out of the body and the potato head began to rot, but Käthe was already moving on to a second experiment. Needing an example of a natural-looking baby's body, she found it in a sculpture of the Christ Child by the fifteenth-century Florentine artist Andrea del Verrocchio. She made a pattern of the body, then sewed it from cotton, filled it with sawdust, and named it Oskar. Like the first doll, Oskar did not have a long life: the sawdust trickled out of his body and left him shapeless, but it didn't matter. Mimerle mothered him with lullabies and love, and Käthe, fascinated by her child's devotion to the crude toy, grew, in her own words, "obsessed with making dolls."

While Käthe was making her first dolls for her children's pleasure, she was also preoccupied with her mother's slow death from tuberculosis. She tended to her mother daily during her final weeks, and when she died, the mourning Käthe wrote in her diary: "My childhood, my past, is gone—my life's work lies ahead of me—my working life."

She continued to experiment with longer-lasting materials to create a doll's body and, realizing at the same time she needed to make a better head, searched for a model to copy that would have the slightly wistful look of a real baby. In 1909 she finally found a bronze bust by the seventeenth-century Belgian artist François Duquesnoy on which to base a doll's head. She covered the model tightly with cloth and poured wax over it, ending up with a shell of a head that could be painted. Her only problem was in creating a proper nose. When she used her method, the noses didn't always end up in the right place on the face and were usually too small or too big. Luckily, she had a source of help in Max, who brought his sculpting experience to the problem. He added a seam to the bridge of the nose, which helped create the snub nose and childlike profile for which Käthe's dolls were to become known.

By the time her third child, Johanna, was born in 1909, after seven years of common-law marriage, Käthe finally agreed to marry Max. Now a more or less conventional—if artistic—family, the husband, wife, and three children moved back to Berlin and tried to lead an ordinary life.

While Käthe had been struggling alone to create a durable, lovable doll, an artistic movement promoting the idea that fine artists should turn their talents to toys—and to dolls in particular—had been growing in both Germany and France. In Germany this movement was centered in Munich and Berlin. An exhibition in 1908 at Munich's Hermann Tietz department store had been organized by the head of the toy department, Max Schreiber. It featured dolls that were meant to look like everyday children rather than the romanticized but stiff porcelain dolls at which Max Kruse had turned up his nose in 1905. In 1910 the Berlin branch of Hermann Tietz planned a similar Christmas exhibition titled *Spielzeug aus eigener Hand* (Self-Made Toys). Because Käthe was the wife of a famous sculptor, her dollmaking efforts were fairly well known, and the store invited her to show some of her dolls in the exhibition. She agreed to create some new ones to display.

The dolls she displayed had hand-painted, molded-cloth heads filled with wax and bodies of nettle cloth (a coarse muslin) filled with wood shavings. While Käthe knew they were not the dolls she dreamed of creating ("I knew exactly what a doll should be like. I also knew exactly how far away I was from my goal," she wrote later), they met with huge success when the exhibition opened. It seemed that everybody who saw them wanted a Käthe Kruse doll. Keeping up with the demand turned the Kruse family life upside down. When a well-known German doll manufacturer, Kammer & Rein-hardt, offered her a contract to manufacture and distribute her designs, it seemed like a good solution. Käthe accepted. In December 1910 she signed the contract and traveled to the factory to begin training the workers. In spite of the many hours she spent training, she proclaimed the first dolls manu-factured by Kammer & Reinhardt completely unacceptable. "They looked like frozen blue flounders with pumped-up limbs," she declared. The heads were hollow and the bodies were too bulky, with awkward joints visible at the knees and neck. Käthe terminated the contract and took back her patterns and molds, bringing produc-tion back into her own home.

A fourth child, son Michel, was born during this period, which grew even more hectic when an order arrived from the famous American toy store FAO Schwarz for 150 dolls to be delivered in November 1911. The Kruse household was overrun with doll parts as Käthe worked to fill the

This beautifully painted boy is an early example of one of Käthe Kruse's earliest dolls, known as Doll I. Standing seventeen inches high, he was made between 1911 and 1914.

order. While caring for her family, she also did everything else—molding heads, stuffing bodies, cutting patterns, and addressing boxes. She hired one painter and five seamstresses. Sometimes things became so chaotic that even Max would lend his hands to the dollmaking venture. The order was successfully completed on time, marking Käthe Kruse's first commercial production of the doll that would come to be known as "Doll I."

Doll I, at seventeen inches high, was very similar to the dolls she had made for the exhibition a year earlier, but the head was now hand-molded of nettle cloth and had a tiny metal nose beneath the molded face mask, which was stuffed with deer hair and wood shavings and sewn onto the back of the head. The heads were primed, sanded, and hand-painted. The minimal hair was also painted on—with one long brown curl on the forehead. The dolls had a sturdy, gentle appearance, with a calm expression and a hint of the awkwardness of a young child's body.

Not until the dolls were packed away on the ship and partway across the ocean did Käthe discover that when the oil paints had run out, her painter had used water-based paints. A single drop of water would turn those lovingly hand-painted faces into a stream of color. After the failure of working with Kammer & Reinhardt and what she saw as her own failure to produce durable dolls, she felt ready to give up. Her dolls were out in the world now, however, and it seemed that the world wanted more of them. Not only were they winning awards at international doll exhibitions in Europe, but FAO Schwarz sent her a new order, forgiving her for the earlier dolls and requesting she make five hundred more.

Käthe had learned some lessons by now. No more turning her home upside down. While on vacation with her family in Bad Kosen, she rented rooms for a workshop. She rehired her painter—with instructions to use the correct paint!—and in the autumn of 1912 began production of a new series of dolls. She registered her Käthe Kruse trademark for the first time. Not long after that, she gave birth to her fifth child, Jochen. (In later years, she had two more boys: Friedebald in 1918 and Max Jr., in 1921.) She thrived on the life of mother

In 1912 Käthe Kruse was the happy mother of four children (from left): Fifi (Sophie), Michel, Hannerle (Johanna), and Mimerle (Maria), the eldest, who unwittingly started her mother's career as a dollmaker.

and businesswoman, nourished and energized by the love of her family and her employees. For Käthe believed that it took a woman—in particular, a mother—to make a true doll for children to play with. When she retired from the business in 1956, leaving it to her children to run, she wrote: "Oh, I hope I'll be forgiven when I say that dolls can only really be made by women. Men's talents are very different from women's. . . . If they try [to make dolls], they end up with dolls that are . . . coquette and dainty, lovely to look at but very inconstant, just like their love."

It required a woman, she held, to create a doll that would bring out the maternal instincts of a child, the deep need to care for another living being. In 1923 she wrote: "My dolls, particularly the babies, arose from the desire to awaken a feeling that one was holding a real baby in one's arms. . . ." To achieve this awakening, she believed, a doll should have a soft, warm body with a natural heaviness.

As she began to work in earnest in her new workshop, she refined her dolls, making the head more oval, painting the hair on its forehead into more of a curl, eliminating some of the seams and stitches. The hands, too, became more sophisticated in design, with longer fingers and a sewn-on thumb. Seven years after her towel-bodied, potato-headed attempt for her daughter, Käthe Kruse was producing endearing chubby-faced, jointed cloth dolls for children of many countries. She was in the doll business.

And her doll business flourished. In 1913 she published her

first catalog of offerings. She continued to refine her original designs as well as to create new ones. During World War I her company manufactured tiny soldier dolls with wire skeletons, which qualified as being supportive of the war effort and allowed the company to stay in business when many other toy companies were forced to close. After the war ended, she began to make dollhouse dolls with the same wire skeletons for posability. In the 1920s she created what she believed was an even more realistic baby doll, which she called *Schlenkerchen* (Floppy Baby), with a new inner construction that allowed the body to bend and the legs to dangle. *Schlenkerchen* was smaller than the original dolls and thus easier for small children to cuddle. She designed the even smaller tiny *Bambino* (Baby), meant to be a doll for a doll or a doll for older girls who could sew and crochet for their dolls.

When Käthe gave birth to her seventh child, Max, her doctor suggested she make a baby doll for new mothers to practice on. Her motherly instincts spurred her imagination into creating a sleeping baby with the weight and proportions of a newborn, which she named *Traumerchen* (Dreaming Baby). Her doctor praised the realistic results, for the baby even had a belly button and a hole in the buttocks so that mothers could practice inserting a thermometer. The doll was greatly sought after for baby-care classes.

When the economy in Germany suffered in 1927, Käthe Kruse responded by creating a smaller, less expensive doll and did so again in 1935. In the late 1920s she made her first doll with a swivel head, based on a sculpture of her eight-year-old son, Friedebald. She made both girl and boy dolls, using the same bodies but giving them different hairstyles and clothing.

While following her heart in making dolls that children could truly love, Käthe Kruse was smart enough to follow her head when it came to business. She fought off other German companies who tried to copy her dolls. She traveled to shops and world fairs, international toy exhibits and trade shows, and advertised widely to help the sales of her dolls. By 1939 her company employed 120 people and made about twelve thousand dolls a year.

The World War II years brought her much personal grief. When Max died, at the age of eighty-eight, in 1942, she lost her best friend. Less than a year later, her son Jochen died of brain cancer. Seven months after Jochen's death, her son Friedebald was killed in a military accident. Within a year and

a half, Käthe lost three of the dearest people in her life.

After the war ended, she and her two remaining sons, Michel and Max, moved the workshop to Donauwörth, farther west in Germany. Her daughters and eight of her employees followed. Working

This circa-1950 doll by Käthe Kruse bears her dolls' trademark wistful face.

alongside their mother, the Kruse children, who had always been involved in some aspects of the dollmaking company, became more and more vital to the business. Käthe maintained her role as spokesperson of the firm, while her children took over much of the company's work. In 1956, when she was seventy-three, Käthe decided to retire, turning over the business to Max, and Hanne and her husband, Heinz Adler. Michel, who was a physicist, had moved to South Africa to pursue his career in 1952, and by 1958 Max, too, left the company to pursue a writing career, leaving Hanne and Heinz in charge. The couple ran the company successfully, holding on to Hanne's motto: "Uphold tradition and build upon our precious inheritance of dollmaking."

Käthe's oldest daughter, Mimerle, who had cared for

This photo of Käthe Kruse surrounded by her company's dolls was taken in 1958, two years after she formally retired from dollmaking.

In 1960 Käthe Kruse posed with a doll and a life-size mannequin, which her company had been making for shop window displays since the 1930s.

Max in his last days, tended to her mother, too, as she aged. On July 19, 1968, just before her eighty-fifth birthday, Käthe Kruse, once a lonely little girl, died surrounded by the love she had created throughout her adulthood. Her death was mourned by her family and friends as well as by all those around the world who loved her dolls.

After her death, the company maintained its solidity artistically and financially under the guidance of Hanne and Heinz. It wasn't until 1990, when Hanne turned eighty, that she decided she was ready for retirement. This time, no family members were interested in running the business, and after a lengthy search for a new owner, a young couple, Stephen and Andrea Christenson, took over the company's operations. Andrea, a native Austrian whose childhood memories are filled with her own Käthe Kruse dolls, brought to her work a fierce devotion to Käthe's original ideals and a determination to maintain the tradition and quality of these classic dolls. Thanks to the guiding spirit of Käthe Kruse's own children and that of the Christensons, Käthe's vision of dolls that inspire tenderness and care flourishes.

"I cannot say I had a happy childhood," Käthe admitted when she was an adult, "and I think it was my own fault." Taking responsibility for her young failures at happiness, Käthe strove to create love and joy in her maturity. In nurturing a large and warm family, she built an emotional and creative foundation for her mission of creating "a child for the child," a mission that bears fruit in many happy children's homes today.

Today the Käthe Kruse company continues to make appealing dolls, though the heads are now vinyl instead of cloth. This trio — (from left) Gepetitto, Lena, and Loltchen — was made in 2001.

Sasha Morgenthaler
(1893–1975)

Born Mary Madeleine Alexandra von Sinner in Bern, Switzerland, in 1893, the girl known as Sasha (a nickname for Alexandra) was a quiet and creative child. She took her first steps at eleven months but barely spoke until she was more than three years old. According to her older sister, Lily, Sasha lived in her own fantasy world, sketching and painting. She played with toy trains, looked after her animals, and climbed the chestnut trees in the lush garden of their first home. She made up and illustrated stories about her dolls and stuffed animals, once scratching off the face of a doll whose smile did not suit her mood. She found the dolls too smotheringly sweet and preferred the company of her favorite pet, Tiny, a Yorkshire terrier who could share her many moods. "I always had a special relationship to animals," Sasha wrote later

Sasha Morgenthaler, shown here as a very young child, barely spoke until she was more than three years old.

in life, "and thanks to my strong fantasy was able to give life to the inanimate objects around me, and soon was also able to express this fantasy in sketches and drawings of many different kinds of figures and forms."

The first eight years of her life she lived in a classic revival villa known as the Schlossli, a Swiss-German word meaning "little palace." Soon after his marriage, her father had bought the magnificent house, which sat in a quiet and elegant part of Bern, surrounded by beautiful gardens. At bedtime Sasha often glimpsed a blue guardian angel outside her bedroom window. After her widowed mother moved the family to a smaller house, Sasha never again saw her blue angel, though it lived vividly in her memory into the last decade of her life, when she rendered it in watercolor. She once said that she had a big hole in her head that swallowed up everything she saw and lived. The dolls she came to create,

Sasha Morgenthaler (right) was the youngest of four children. This photo shows her with her sister Lily and brother Kurt.

too, seem to hold infinite experiences within.

The youngest of four children, Sasha never knew her father, Edward, a Swiss aristocrat who died less than a year after her birth. Her mother, Marie, an unconventional, well-educated Jewish woman from Berlin, Germany, kept the von Sinner household filled with the lively stimulation of constant guests: musicians, scientists, social thinkers, writers, and artists. Among them was the painter Paul Klee, who would eventually become a famous artist. At the time when Sasha was a girl, though, he liked to come to the von Sinner house with his wife to play chamber music. He played the violin and viola; his wife played the piano.

When Sasha was nine, Klee noticed her drawings and began to encourage her in her artwork. He tried to bring her artistic abilities to her mother's attention, but Marie von Sinner was much more interested in music and literature than in the visual arts. Still, Klee's attention cheered the girl. Very likely, too, she enjoyed the puppets that Klee made for his son, Felix, from scraps of cloth, paintbrushes, and other odds and ends. For in spite of the lively household, Sasha was lonely. Her mother believed strongly in education for women. In 1904, at the age of thirty-seven, she herself began to study medicine, and she made sure that much of Sasha's time was spent with private tutors, preparing for her high school entrance. The young girl, however, was as uninterested in academics as her mother was in art and, in fact, often feigned illness to avoid her studies and eventually school, where she was the only girl in her class.

"She pretended a heart ailment," her sister Lily recalled, "and managed with great skill to produce a high temperature, convincing the doctors of her delicate state of health. In that way she achieved the privilege of being left in peace and quiet. She thoroughly enjoyed her months in bed: read, carved designs in wood, painted, and sketched." Sasha wanted to be a sculptor or a painter. Klee's attention gave her hope that she might have an artistic future.

Fourteen years older than Sasha and twelve years younger than her mother, Klee was a good intermediary between the two strong and opposing personalities. When Sasha turned sixteen, he finally convinced Marie to send the talented teen-ager to the Geneva Academy of Art. In 1909 Sasha, having "recovered her health," went off to pursue her artistry.

She spent five years studying painting in Geneva. She had

always been one to paint exactly what her keen eyes perceived, and in her studies she continued to base her work on her direct observations of nature. In 1914 Klee, still her staunch supporter and adviser, arranged for her to train under the painter Cuno Amiet in the farming village of Oschwand. Amiet was known for his simple and direct visual style, which was in keeping with Sasha's own interest in realistic renditions of people and objects but in opposition to the craze for abstraction and expressionism that was sweeping Europe at the time. Amiet's students stayed in a picturesque inn with brightly colored shutters and window boxes filled with flowers, separated from his home and studio by luxurious gardens. It was in this quiet village that Sasha first came to know the man she would eventually marry, the realist painter Ernst Morgenthaler. Ernst was also studying with Cuno Amiet, and Sasha's early admiration for Ernst's work may have been what first attracted her to her future husband.

Again with Klee's help, she moved to Germany later that year to study sculpture at the Holoshi School in Munich. He encouraged her to take an anatomy class to help her sculpting effort—a very unusual step for a woman with artistic aspirations in that era. Klee's suggestion played an important part in Sasha's future work, for the study of anatomy not only gave her a firm technical foundation for her sculpting but was also crucial to her eventual understanding of dollmaking.

When Sasha arrived in Munich, she found a city throbbing with artistic activity. She came into contact with many avant-garde artists, who were promoting new, often shocking ideas. Most important among them were Wassily Kandinsky and Franz Marc. Kandinsky, though a reserved and conventional-looking man, was a leader of the movement that turned its back on figurative art—art that depicted objects, people, and scenes very realistically—in favor of abstract designs of shapes and colors. Kandinsky proclaimed that a piece of abstract art did not merely *show* an image but *was* an image. Kandinsky and Marc were founders of a movement known as the Blaue Reiter (Blue Rider), which championed abstraction. Unlike some artistic movements, however, which can be single-minded in their adherence to a particular philosophy, the Blaue Reiter encouraged any means of artistic expression as worthwhile.

The avant-garde obsession with abstraction did not much interest Sasha, who continued to concentrate on her realistic style, even as she was brought into the circle by Paul Klee and Ernst Morgenthaler, who by that time had also come to Munich. In spite of her focus on the figurative, Sasha felt artistically at home in this group. She was lucky that, unlike many female artists in earlier times, her creative work was encouraged and fostered by those around her. The open-minded approach of the Blaue Reiter movement surely had an influence on Sasha's later work with dolls.

In 1916 Sasha married Ernst Morgenthaler, and the couple returned to Switzerland, living first in Geneva. Though she painted briefly after her marriage, soon Sasha gave up her painting and sculpture to become a full-time wife and mother. Her decision was formed by her conviction that there could be only one artist in the family, and she let her husband take that role.

Even though Sasha had given up a formal artistic career when she married, her aesthetic sensibility was always evident in the Morgenthaler homes. The family moved several times, and each of their dwellings, though furnished simply on an artist's income, was marked by Sasha's creativity. Her first son, Niklaus, who was born in 1918, remembers how his mother painted their plain pinewood beds light blue — the color of dreams. Perhaps she was remembering the blue guardian angel of her childhood?

A second son, Fritz, was born in 1919. In 1920 the family moved to Zurich, and in 1924 their third child, Barbara, was born. With Barbara's birth, the first stuffed animals and dolls began to emerge from Sasha's hands. "The toys for sale in the stores were too expensive," Sasha explained later, "and in addition I didn't like them." She brought her trained artistic sensibility and technique to the earliest of her creations, a gray-and-white-spotted cat, which led to more exotic species: zebras, lions, peacocks. The animals were simply constructed from cloth and wire into primitive and cuddly, but immediately recognizable, shapes and characters. They were seemingly expressionless, a reaction, no doubt, to Sasha's great disdain for the grinning dolls of her childhood. Their personalities came from their construction and pose. Barbara recalled:

"On the dinner table in the living room, Mother sculpted cloth and wire into animals. I marveled at how the camel came to life. The water buffalo frightened me a little. For every meal the table had to be cleared and set with tablecloth and flowers."

Toymaking was just one part of Sasha's life, though, in the first few decades of her marriage. In 1933 she created clever hand puppets to go with verses Ernst had written for a reception of important Swiss artists. In 1934 she went to train as a midwife at the women's hospital in the town of Basel, many miles away, leaving her children and Ernst in the care of their young housekeeper for nearly a year so that she might have a profession independent of the arts. (After she had been gone some time, her family sent her a letter that read—in a paraphrase of the *Snow White* rhyme "mirror, mirror, on the wall"— "fried egg, fried egg, on the plate, are you the only food in the land?")

When she returned from Basel, she began to make life-size plaster mannequins, which were widely displayed in Switzerland and abroad. When World War II broke out, Sasha founded the Women's Aid Auxiliary Troops, which assisted in transporting refugees, forced to leave their homelands due to the war, to other countries. Her fierce, compassionate nature made her a powerful force in keeping families together in these tragic circumstances. The undertones of emotion she saw in the expressions of children she met during those years found their way onto the faces of the dolls she soon began to create.

In 1941 Sasha won first prize in the toy competition of the Swiss Federation. "Mother made a little duck that rolled across the table," Barbara described. "She painted it blue and white, the colors of Zurich, and sent it to a competition for an emblem of the Swiss Show in Zurich. She got first prize. The rolling little ducks appeared everywhere." Soon after receiving this award, Sasha turned to dollmaking in earnest. Her inability to find affordable and appealing dolls for her children had fostered her determination to create a sensitive, durable, and inexpensive play doll. Her own study of painting and sculpture, together with her observations of her husband's portraiture, had brought her to understand that it was the asymmetrical quality of the human face—the fact that each half of a face was different from the other half—that gave a person his or her individuality. From Ernst's portraiture, she also learned that she could bring a face to life with simple quick strokes. It is easy to see this influence

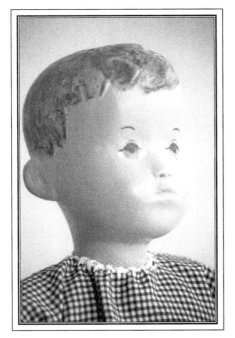

Sasha Morgenthaler made this boy doll in the early 1940s. He has a cloth body and his hair is molded, which is typical of Sasha's very early dolls.

This Eskimo Girl and Boy were made by Sasha Morgenthaler in 1961. Her travels inspired her to make dolls representing a wide variety of ethnic groups.

when you look at the sparsely painted face of a Sasha doll. She learned, too, from a close friend, the sculptor Karl Geiser, about representing the parts of the body with simple shapes that were recognizable due to their proportions, and put this knowledge to use. In her dolls, Sasha was finally able to bring together her lifelong interest in realistic portrayal with the best principles of the abstract artistic movement she had experienced.

She first tried to make the heads of wax, hoping to achieve the tautness and transparency of youthful skin. The bodies were a stuffed cotton knit. Both media were eventually used, along with a variety of others. Most of the dolls were about twenty inches high; their skin tones ranged from very pale to a soft dark cast. They wore wigs of natural hair, and their clothing was always muted and harmonious in color. In fact, most often, the color Sasha chose was white.

She designed all the clothing, rarely using new fabrics, preferring soft, worn cloth. She searched flea markets in

Switzerland for materials. Later in her life, as she began to travel frequently throughout the world, she acquired old fabrics wherever she went, and her dolls came to represent a wide range of ethnic children in dress and hairstyle.

In 1943 she brought together a small team, including plasterers, seamstresses, and wigmakers, who worked with her to produce dolls as the demand for her unique playthings grew. Sasha experimented and struggled to achieve her technical goals. In 1944 she and her team introduced all-wax dolls made from six pieces, displaying them at an exhibition in the city of Zurich's Museum of Applied Arts. Her goal was to have dolls ready to sell at the Heimatwerk, a handicraft shop in Zurich, for the Christmas 1945 season. The completed dolls, displayed in the store windows in a delightful scene, drew many shoppers. Customers wrapped in blankets to guard against the biting Swiss winter air lined up in front of the shop the night

before the dolls went on sale. People had never seen anything like Sasha's dolls, and they wanted them regardless of the price.

Sasha developed a basic face, with four variations, for her dolls representing older children as well as another variation for the

Sasha made this doll, part of a group known as the Bauernkinder (farm children), in 1965.

babies and toddlers. She strove to give the faces a peaceful gaze, with only the illusion of expression; they were to be non-nationalistic, simple, and harmonious. She wanted to achieve a face capable of many moods so that every child could read into her own doll the expression she needed to find there. "It is the interplay of asymmetry in the proportions that creates a lively effect," she explained. "The asymmetrical construction of the doll, which must at the same time create a unified whole, is the basis for the numerous possibilities of expression in my dolls."

She eventually achieved a successful asymmetrical body in the late 1940s. It was made of a synthetic resin, a forerunner of hard plastic (which soon became the standard medium for dolls). Sasha continued, however, to use different media, including all plaster and cloth, for the dolls' bodies through the late 1960s. She came to achieve all her goals but one: the dolls were still so expensive that only the wealthiest children could play with them.

In her relentless hope to produce less-expensive dolls, she turned to the German toy company Götz in 1963 and allowed them to produce her doll designs in their factory. These dolls are beautiful and rare

Representing a "Girl of 1900," this doll made by Sasha in 1969 bears the enigmatic expression that characterizes the artist's work.

Two years before she died, Sasha created this doll, which she called "Black Girl of Today." It bears the number 56/073, meaning it was the fifty-sixth doll she made in 1973.

today. But they did not meet Sasha's standards and, disappointed, she stopped their production.

In 1965 she met an English couple, John and Sara Doggart, who owned a toy company called Trendon in the north of England. The Doggarts had been searching for years for a doll design that was, as they said, different from "the humdrum sort of creatures which we, as well as everybody else, were then producing." When they saw a photograph of one of Sasha's dolls in a Swiss magazine, the Doggarts explained: "We sent a telegram to Mrs. Morgenthaler and hopped on a plane to Zurich." But after her experience with Götz, Sasha was reluctant to let her designs be produced by anybody else. "She was not at all keen to let us use her design," the Doggarts recalled. "She was suspicious of commerce." The couple convinced her of their love and respect for her dolls, and eventually Sasha agreed to let them try their hand at production.

The dolls the Doggarts produced remained true to the originals' body design, neutral face, and simple harmonious clothing and pleased the artist. Later Sasha wrote: "Because with the help of my friends the Doggarts it became possible to pro-

Gregor in Pyjamas is an example of the successful Sasha dolls produced by the English Trendon company. He was made between 1968 and 1970.

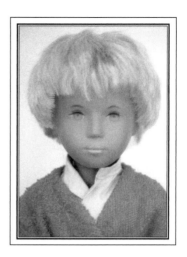

duce inexpensive dolls which meet my expectations, I can presume to spend the last years of my life realizing my dream, perhaps to create dolls that arouse feelings of approval, love, and humanity."

After her death in 1975, the Doggarts continued to uphold her standards. "Now I am dressing the doll—very carefully," Sara Doggart said after Sasha's death, "considering what Sasha Morgenthaler might have wanted. She and I had a good accord and when I am pleased with a new outfit, I wish that she could see it and enjoy it with me. . . . I love this doll and dress her as I would dress a child." The Doggarts continued to manufacture inexpensive, sixteen-inch-high vinyl Sashas with rooted hair, which became, as Sasha had envisioned, the beloved playmates of a generation of children. In 1986, however, production of the English Sashas ended when the Doggarts retired without finding anyone capable of carrying on production to their standards.

But those who loved Sasha dolls could not let the artist's dreams die with the Doggarts' retirement. A few years after the Doggarts closed down their company, an American named

Stephen Miller, who had come to be a friend of Sasha's when he owned a toy shop in New York City's Greenwich Village, obtained permission to produce dolls from the old molds. Sadly, he died of cancer in 1993, before production could get under way. In 1995 the original manufacturer of Sasha's dolls, the German company Götz, was awarded the license to produce the dolls. For six years Sashas were again seen on toy store shelves, in children's arms, and in the arms of collectors, many of whom remember the dolls from their own childhoods. In 2001, however, the Sasha Morgenthaler estate decided it was no longer happy with Götz's production and took away the company's license. The search continues for a manufacturer to once more produce this enigmatic, magical Mona Lisa of dolls.

Beatrice Alexander Behrman

(1895–1990)

 *The feisty, ambitious girl who would* become known to the world as Madame Alexander was born on March 9, 1895, in Brooklyn, New York. The oldest daughter of poor, hardworking Russian immigrants, she grew up on New York City's Lower East Side in a crowded and bustling neighborhood, where her parents owned the country's first doll hospital. Bertha, as she was known throughout her childhood and early adulthood, and her three younger sisters, Rose, Florence, and Jean, lived with their parents over the Alexander Doll Hospital on Grand Street, their home marked by a blue sign with a white cross. Like all their neighbors, they struggled daily to make ends meet. Bertha's stepfather, Maurice, repaired the porcelain dolls wealthy, brokenhearted girls brought to him; her mother, Hannah, after a long day of

This hand-painted miniature of young Bertha Alexander is the only known photograph of her as a child.

household chores, washed the dolls and combed out tangles in their hair.

Maurice and Hannah had both arrived in the United States during the 1890s, along with two million other Jewish immigrants who had come to make their home in New York City in the late nineteenth and early twentieth centuries. Most of them were from Eastern European countries, fleeing the Russian pogroms, massacres of the Jewish population, that were instigated and supported by Russia's ruler, Czar Alexander III. Maurice Alexander had been a young student when he left Russia for Germany, where he swept floors for a man who repaired mechanical dolls, clocks, and china. His employer taught Maurice his trade and gave him a letter of introduction to a colleague in the United States—a head start for a young man in a new country. Austrian-born Hannah Pepper, who had been living in Russia during the pogroms, managed to escape directly to America.

The world in which Maurice and Hannah found themselves raising their daughters was one of streets teeming with the noises and smells of people living and working together much too closely, all of them trying to build a better life for themselves and their families. "It was a ghetto," Bertha's daughter, Mildred, would later describe, "where people lived on top of one another." The neighborhood echoed with the sounds of the Yiddish language that united the Jewish immigrants as well as with Polish, Russian, German, and other native tongues of Eastern Europe.

Throughout her childhood, Bertha watched, day after day, as elegant horse-drawn carriages pulled up to the doll hospital and beautifully dressed young girls emerged, usually in tears, clutching a broken porcelain doll. Her heart ached for them, even as she envied their clothes and carriages. "Someday," she told her mother when she was twelve years old, "I am going to make beautiful dolls that don't break!" At the same time, she vowed silently to herself that someday she, too, would have a carriage and a hat with ostrich feathers. "When I was eleven or twelve," Madame Alexander recalled later in life, "I realized that there were poor people and there were rich people, and I leaned towards the rich." Even as a very young child, she had an eye for the best and could be captivated by a delicate Dresden porcelain figurine.

By her own accounts, Bertha was the "difficult" child. She liked to tell the story of her mother waking her one evening to satisfy the whim of a wealthy customer who wanted to play with her. The lady held Bertha and played with one of her long sausage curls, stretching it out and letting it snap back against the six-year-old's head. Sleepy Bertha soon had enough of this game and slapped the woman. Her mother was scandalized, fearing she'd lost a customer, and began to scold her daughter. "But my father stepped in and said, 'Hannah, you are not to scold her,'" Madame would relate. "'She has character, and someday the world will hear of her.'" Though Maurice had married Hannah when Bertha was a very small child, the bond between stepfather and stepdaughter was so strong that she never referred to him as anything but her father. (In fact, she was never told who her biological father was.) For his part, Maurice had an innate understanding of Bertha and a prophetic sense of her potential; her strength, energy, ambition, and outspokenness only increased as she grew older and were the very traits that helped her persevere at times when others might have given up.

Bertha saw her father as an idealist and her mother as the practical parent. Practical as her mother was, though, she was also a lover of beauty and kept the simple apartment above the doll hospital filled with beautiful objects. She turned the little bit of land behind the shop into a restful garden, where her family could escape for brief respites from the tedium of their daily tasks. Bertha loved to read among the greenery and the flowers, immersing herself in classics like Lewis Carroll's *Alice in Wonderland*, Charles Dickens's *David Copperfield*, and her favorite—being one of four sisters in a financially struggling family—Louisa May Alcott's *Little Women*. She also inherited her mother's love of beauty, especially when it came to clothes. Promised a new holiday dress one year, Bertha insisted on shopping at a fancy department store. "We walked in the door and all the sales clerks were lined up in a row, and mumbling in astonishment when they saw us. But we marched on and saw three wonderful dresses. My mother said, 'Which one?' 'All three,' I said. And they bought them for me! My father went to services with his old hat cleaned and his shoes resoled, and I had my new dresses."

With three sisters following behind her, the three dresses were guaranteed to get a lot of wear, and it was lucky for Rose, Florence, and Jean that their oldest sister had such good taste. Like Maurice, Hannah prophesied about Bertha, but without accounting for the girl's independent spirit. "My mother used to say it was going to take three husbands to support me!" Madame remembered. Instead, it would be Bertha who would support herself—and her family—in the style to which she aspired.

Though they may have differed in temperament, her idealist father and practical mother were united in their aspirations for their daughters and in their insistence on education as the first step toward a better life. Bertha was an excellent student as well as a gifted artist and won many honors, including, when she was sixteen, a scholarship to study sculpting in Paris. The scholarship, rather than being a source of joy, became one of disappointment, as she was not allowed to accept it. The bank in which her parents had kept their money had failed, and their life savings were gone. Her family could not send her abroad.

Unhappy but undaunted in her pursuit of greater achievements, she persisted at her academics and was class valedictorian when she graduated from Washington Irving High School the following year, in 1912. Her achievements in art were awarded by a complete set of Shakespeare's plays. But Bertha had not spent her youth devoted solely to academics and art; there was romance in her life, too. A few weeks after graduation, on June 30, she married her steady beau, Philip Behrman. "I was able to become what I became because of Philip and his love and support of me," she acknowledged more than sixty years later.

Philip worked in the personnel department of a local hat factory, and Bertha took a well-paying bookkeeping job at Irving Hat Stores. For a few years they led the fairly typical life of a young, happily married couple of the time. In 1915 their daughter, Mildred, was born, and Bertha found new joy in motherhood. "The happiest moment of my life," she rhapsodized when she was ninety-three, "was when I opened my eyes and saw my baby next to me." She could not deny, however, the growing need for a creative life. The opportunity to revive her artistic nature—and to test her entrepreneurial spirit—came during the later years of World War I.

At the Alexander Doll Hospital, Maurice Alexander not only repaired broken porcelain dolls, he also sold beautiful new ones. Like most toys of high quality played with by wealthy American children in the late nineteenth and early twentieth centuries, these luxurious dolls were imported from Europe, and especially from Germany. With the outbreak of World War I in 1914, German factories had to stop producing non-necessities, such as toys, in favor of war supplies. As the years went on and war continued to be waged, the supply of toys in the United States dwindled. The shelves of the Alexander Doll Hospital, like those of most American toy shops, grew empty. Maurice and Hannah not only had no dolls to sell, they were equally hard put to make any repairs. Doll parts, also made in Germany, were in short supply.

Bertha had strong memories from her childhood above the doll hospital of the importance of a doll for children. "Dolls are not a luxury," she was to say decades later. "They are as necessary to a child's life as a loaf of bread." Now that she had her own small daughter, those memories grew especially vivid. Worried, too, about her family's income and never one to wallow in emotion when she could act, she came up with a plan. She would make dolls—unbreakable, of course—for her parents to sell in the shop. Enlisting the help of her three sisters, she designed a Red Cross nurse doll, in commemoration of the brave women tending to the sick and wounded in the war. She stitched it from muslin and stuffed it with excelsior—a soft mixture of long, thin wood shavings commonly used for stuffing plush animals. As soon as they hit the store shelves, the Red Cross nurses were a success.

Thrilled with having created something so clearly needed, Bertha went on to make a realistic baby doll and tested it on little Mildred, who remembers it looked so real that her mother even bought a baby bottle for it. Now Bertha knew she had found a direction for her ambition and energy. "Necessity is the mother of invention," she reiterated in the 1980s. "There was a need for American children to have dolls, and we filled that need." As she designed other cloth dolls, she would offer the first sample to her mother and sisters for critique, then would teach them how to re-create it. While she was capable of making the sample, Bertha recognized that her talent lay not in sewing but in knowing what she wanted—and how to direct other people to construct it. "I'm not a seamstress," she once said. "I just created the dolls, and fortunately had people who were able to make my dreams." Her three sisters would sit for hours around the kitchen table in the Grand Street apartment, stitching and painting under Bertha's watchful eye. "That was my first training for becoming an executive," she explained later.

A portrait of little Mildred was the next commercial success, inspiring Bertha, in 1923, to officially found the Alexander Doll Company. She obtained a loan of $1,600, which enabled her to hire neighborhood men and women who came after work every night to join the sewing circle in the Grand Street apartment. Shopkeepers came with baskets to collect as many dolls as they wanted, which they would sell for $1.98

each. Eventually the business thrived enough that she could rent a separate studio for $40 a month.

For creative inspiration, Bertha turned to the books she had loved as a child. Her early dolls represented Alice in Wonderland, Dickens characters like Tiny Tim and David Copperfield, and the four sisters who had captured her young heart: the Little Women. In the first years of the business, the dolls had flat cloth faces with painted features. After a few years she found a way to shape the face and make the features three-dimensional, discovering on her own a traditional method of molding a stiff mask that would be covered by felt or muslin: "I wet some buckram and stretched it over a bowl and pushed it and let it dry, until my dolls could have a proper face with a nose and cheeks and a mouth." She learned of a new, supposedly indestructible material for dolls called composition, which was literally a mixture—a composition—of sawdust, resin, and papier-mâché, and began buying composition-bodied dolls for her employees to costume. Eventually Bertha, always frustrated by not being in control, would take over the process of manufacturing the composition dolls in addition to her cloth dolls, but for the first few years, she bought the unclothed bodies from other manufacturers.

The mix of practicality and romanticism she had inherited from her parents characterized her throughout her life. As her company began to grow, she immersed herself in the decidedly unromantic business details and in the magic of the stories and characters she brought to life. Caught up in the dreams of beauty she wanted her dolls to instill in children, she even renamed herself, leaving Bertha behind for the more romantic Beatrice. Eventually she took on the title of Madame, perhaps to carry out her childhood fantasies of elegance and aristocracy. It was as Madame Alexander that the world came to "hear of her," as her stepfather, Maurice, had predicted, and the allure of a Madame Alexander doll became all the more desirable due to that self-bestowed title.

Before she could attain the success and respect she strove for, however, Madame experienced frequent frustration and discouragement as her young business suffered the growing pains of any fledgling endeavor. She regularly ran out of money and, accompanied by young Mildred for moral support, would visit bankers and plead for loans—which she usually received. Sometimes, Madame recalled, "I was desperate, discouraged. I wanted to run away, but by then I had employees, sixteen people who depended on me."

One of her lowest moments must have been the day her factory flooded. Mildred, who had come to work that day with her mother and grandmother Hannah, remembers the disaster vividly. "We walked in one morning and found the whole factory floating in four feet of water—the water tower on top of the building had broken and flooded everything. My grandmother, who was as full of energy as my mother, waded in and began gathering as many little dresses as she could, took them home, wrung them out, and hung them everywhere to dry. 'We'll have a water sale,' she decided, threw open the doors with everything marked way down, and earned just enough money to keep the company in business." Practical Hannah had saved the day.

Madame had her own approach to saving her company. One especially grim morning, she packed up her favorite Little Women dolls and, convinced that public attention would revive her business, talked her way into an interview with the well-known newspaper writer Mary Margaret McBride, whose column in the *World Telegram* was widely read. Once she had the columnist's ear, Beatrice, spinning her tale in her romantic fashion, enthralled McBride. The result was a half-page article in the newspaper that told the inspiring story of Madame Beatrice Alexander and her dolls. The final line was one that Madame loved to quote for decades to come: "Not only does Madame Alexander put soles on her dolls, but she puts souls into them!" As she had hoped, the resulting publicity brought a new burst of orders to her company.

Enterprising actions like these sustained and nurtured the Alexander Doll Company. By the 1930s Madame had hit her stride, and she never lost it. Since the success of her first Red Cross nurse doll, she had come to realize that she had a talent for understanding what the public wanted. She had an instinct for gauging—and sometimes predicting—people's insatiable fascination with a particular movie star or celebrity and acted swiftly to satisfy it. When in 1933 RKO Studios released the film *Little Women* starring famous box office stars Katharine

In 1949 Madame Alexander created a group of fourteen-inch Little Women dolls based on the characters from the movie released that year. The hard-plastic dolls represent (from left) Meg, Beth, Jo, Amy, and Marmee.

Hepburn and Joan Bennett, Madame promptly applied for and received a trademark to produce sixteen-inch cloth renditions of the March sisters. (Since 1933 there have always been Little Women—including, later, patient Marmee and neighbor Laurie—in the Alexander Doll Company line. When a new film of the book was produced in 1949, Madame created the characters in hard plastic.) When the world hailed the birth of the first surviving quintuplets in Canada as a modern-day miracle, Madame was quick to obtain the license to manufacture doll renditions of the Dionnes in 1935. She made the most of her success by producing the dolls in various versions and sizes. As the fascinated world watched the sisters grow from babyhood to girlhood, Madame ensured that toddler dolls followed the baby dolls.

In 1937 she capitalized on the two international obsessions

of the year. The first was the MGM movie version of Margaret Mitchell's novel *Gone with the Wind*. Madame, who had spent a long sleepless night in 1936 reading *Gone with the Wind* in one sitting, fell under the spell of the impetuous heroine, Scarlett O'Hara. She later told reporters: "On Monday morning, after finishing the book, I went to work, and by Wednesday, I had created a doll from the description of Scarlett in the novel. She had a heart-shaped face, a small nose, green eyes, black hair, and was one of my prettiest doll characters." Two years later MGM would cast green-eyed, black-haired Vivien Leigh in the unforgettable role of Scarlett O'Hara, and the Alexander Doll Company would have the license to produce the doll. Like the Little Women, Scarlett became one of the staple characters in almost every year of the company's production.

The second object of the world's fascination in 1937 was the eleven-year-old daughter of England's newly crowned King George VI, Princess Elizabeth, who herself would one day sit on England's throne. In honor of the coronation, the Alexander Doll Company created a Princess Elizabeth doll and continued to use the same face on dolls throughout the coming decades—including Snow White, which was also introduced that year in conjunction with the Walt Disney cartoon.

Thanks to her perseverance, creativity, and ambition, Madame Alexander pulled her company through the difficult struggles of its first decade, which included the Great Depression of 1929 and the early 1930s, a time when many older and more established businesses failed. By the mid-1930s her company had a firm place of stature in the toy industry. In 1936 the business magazine *Fortune* published an article about the three most important American doll companies of the era, and the Alexander Doll Company was selected as one of the three, along with Madame's primary competitors, Effanbee and Ideal. Recognition by *Fortune* was acknowledgment not only of Madame's creative genius but also of her steady guidance of the nuts and bolts of the business. She kept a careful eye on quality control of the dolls and their costumes, ensured that her company shipped dolls to customers on schedule and in the right quantities, and supported the stores' sales with advertising and special events. Always at Madame's side was her husband, Philip Behrman, whom she had persuaded, under threat of divorce, years earlier to leave his job as the personnel manager of a large firm and work with her. In her nineties Madame could still recall the moment when she first asked Philip to leave his job. "I'll never forget the look on his face when he said, 'Are you out of your mind? We have to make a living.' This became such a fixation with me—nothing could get in the way of my dream—that I finally said to him, 'It seems to me I can always get another man.'"

In spite of her single-minded, feminist approach to her business, at home Madame struggled to maintain the life of wife and mother. "After a day's work, I shopped, I cleaned, I cooked. God gave me good health. My daughter was a very dear child, an easy child. She said, 'Mother, I know what you're doing.'" A neighbor usually stayed with young Mildred until Madame came home—sometimes as late as midnight. Unapologetic, unregretful, but honest, in her later life Madame reflected, "I made a big sacrifice. I gave up many things I would have enjoyed."

In the 1940s Madame continued to add famous celebrities to her doll line, while never failing to include the dolls she knew little girls would always want: princesses, storybook characters, walking dolls, baby dolls, and even stuffed animals. Her company, which had outgrown several locations over its twenty years of existence, now had its office and factory on East 24th Street in Manhattan, while its showroom was a few blocks away in the internationally known Toy Center at 200 Fifth Avenue.

The World War II years brought renewed wartime challenges of reduced supplies and rationing of necessary materials. But Madame was not disheartened. It had been, after all, during the last world war that she had been inspired to create her first doll. It was almost as though she thrived on hardship. Despite limited materials, she insisted on maintaining the quality of her dolls and their clothing. And then it was, in fact, a wartime technological development that helped pave the way to one of Madame's greatest achievements: the pioneering of a new unbreakable material that revolutionized not only dollmaking but the entire toy industry.

During the war a new material had been put into use that could be easily molded while it was soft, then set firmly in place. Moisture and temperature changes did not affect its surface. Today we cannot imagine a world without plastic, but in the 1940s it was virtually unknown for household use. Toys were made of wood, cloth, porcelain, pressed steel, tinplate, and composition. Although one of Madame's competitors, the Ideal Toy & Novelty Company, apparently manufactured a plastic doll in 1940, they were forced to discontinue it due to wartime restrictions on the use of plastic. Plastic was used in the various military services, to repair airplanes, for example, and when the war ended, toy companies began experimenting with this miraculous material. From 1947 to 1949 Madame's husband, Philip, worked closely with chemical engineers to help develop a plastic formula that would be especially well suited to doll production. In 1947 the Alexander Doll Company began to produce its first hard-plastic dolls, setting an example that the other doll manufacturers would follow.

The new medium ushered in what Alexander doll lovers refer to as Madame's Golden Age of Dolls. As the 1940s turned into the 1950s, the Alexander Doll Company began to create some of the most glamorous dolls the twentieth century had ever seen. Not only was Madame one of the first doll manufacturers to embrace plastic, she set unmatchable standards in the beauty of the dolls' face painting and their exquisite costuming. In fact, it became clear during this time that Madame's greatest creative talent was as a clothing designer. The postwar Alexander dolls wore stunning ensembles that equaled the fashions worn by wealthy women and girls of this prosperous decade. In the 1957 catalog, a typical costume description

The fashion doll known as Cissy made her debut in 1955. She was twenty-one inches high and had a glamorous wardrobe, beginning with her elegant lingerie and high heels.

read: "Elise wearing . . . a chocolate brown velvet coat, lined with pink taffeta, worn over a pink taffeta dress [and] a cocoa brown hat trimmed with pale pink roses." In 1955, four years before Mattel introduced the eleven-and-a-half-inch fashion doll known as Barbie, Madame created a twenty-one-inch full-figured fashion doll, Cissy, who came in a "chemise of lace, long nylon hose, and mules trimmed with lace and flowers." Separate elegant ensembles could be purchased for her. As always, Madame believed she was doing more than just selling a doll; she was teaching young girls good grooming and good taste. "A child should see at an early age how important it is to wear well-fitting clothes in becoming colors," she declared.

Perhaps the truest proof of the outstanding quality of her dolls' clothing was the acknowledgment she received from the world of fashion. In the 1950s the fashion industry paid

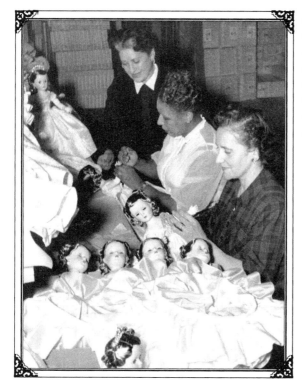

Madame Alexander oversaw every step of the production of the dolls created to celebrate the 1953 coronation of England's Queen Elizabeth II.

homage to her talent by awarding her the Fashion Academy's gold medal on four separate occasions. This top honor was normally presented to fashion designers who created full-size clothing, but the academy recognized Madame, stating that by "dressing Alexander dolls in clothes that are lovely in fabric and exquisite in design, you have not alone made them enchanting and precious in themselves, but you have helped to stimulate in our younger generation an exciting interest in fashion and a growing awareness of style. For reflecting the ultimate in design beauty, for encouraging good taste and clothes appreciation, and for symbolizing 'best dressed' so

perfectly, Alexander dolls are truly deserving of this tribute."
The *Christian Science Monitor* newspaper called Alexander dolls
the "Cadillacs of dolldom."

During that decade one of Madame Alexander's early subjects came to the international forefront again, and Madame
celebrated her glory with her. The coronation of England's
Queen Elizabeth in 1953 was commemorated worldwide, and
Madame personally oversaw the construction of a thirty-six-
doll set that re-created the entire pageant of the coronation.
The dolls were authentically costumed down to their under-
clothing, and six tableaux were built and decorated to match
the various settings of the coronation ceremony. The entire
grouping was exhibited at the Abraham & Straus department

*The Cherry Twins, first made in 1957, were among the popular
eight-inch hard-plastic dolls girls played with in the late 1950s
and early 1960s.*

store in Brooklyn, where it drew thousands of visitors a day in the week preceding the coronation.

By the 1960s Madame had achieved—perhaps surpassed— her vision of being a legend. Her dolls were loved by little girls worldwide. The United Nations honored her in 1965. That same year the Smithsonian Institution in Washington, D.C., placed two of her dolls in its permanent collection. And her company continued to thrive. Even as the culture of the 1960s underwent radical change and Barbie came to rule the world of dolls, Madame continued to insist on traditional beautiful dolls that a girl could nurture. When feminists protested that playing with dolls fostered inappropriate ambitions for young girls, Madame responded: "It is ridiculous to say that a doll makes a little girl have a false image of herself. What a doll does for a little girl is develop her capacity to love others and herself." It is very likely that she spoke from a deeply held memory of the tearful girls with their broken dolls who had come to her family's doll hospital more than sixty years earlier.

With her unbreakable dolls, Madame Alexander had brought happiness to several generations of girls since that time. Many who had grown up with her dolls had become adults and were avidly collecting the dolls they had loved to near destruction, discarded, or never had the opportunity to own. The Madame Alexander Fan Club was formed in 1961, and Madame became the subject of numerous tributes. Over the next few decades, as children and collectors competed for dolls, sometimes there simply weren't enough to go around. Stores began to limit sales of Alexander dolls to one per customer. Wherever Madame appeared—at a store or an event—crowds followed. When Disneyland and Disney World opened in 1955 and 1971, respectively, special events were held for Alexander doll lovers. After one particularly hectic day of ticket sales to a Madame Alexander dinner, a Disney World spokesperson declared her "more popular than Elvis."

This circa-1950s publicity photo shows the very successful Madame Alexander, flanked by some of her favorite dolls of the era.

In 1986, when she was ninety-one, FAO Schwarz named her the First Lady of Dolls, in acknowledgment of her more than fifty years of doll sales at the store. Even then Madame was still closely involved in the workings of her company. Philip had died in 1966, and her son-in-law, Richard, had helped her run the company until his retirement in the early 1980s. From that time on, Madame's grandson, William (Bill) Birnbaum, directed the company with her. In 1988, when Madame turned ninety-three, she finally, reluctantly, came to realize that she and Bill could no longer sustain the company's growth on their own. She sold the Alexander Doll Company and retired to Palm Beach, Florida, where she died, at the age of ninety-five, on October 3, 1990. Today the Alexander Doll factory in the Harlem neighborhood of New York City continues Madame's legacy of creating beautiful, unbreakable dolls, proving that a girl with a dream need only add determination, creativity, and perseverance to make it come true.

The ten-inch-high Poppy Garden Ball Gown doll was in the 2002 collection produced by the Alexander Doll Company.

Ruth Handler

(1916–2002)

A self-proclaimed tomboy, Ruth Mosko Handler steered clear of dolls when she was a girl. Her favorite playmates were her older brothers Muzzy and Aaron. But her favorite pastime, by the age of ten, was what her husband, Elliot, called "a grown-up activity." "Ruthie loved to work," recalled brother Aaron, and Ruth confirmed this in her autobiography, *Dream Doll.* "I simply preferred working over playing with other kids," she wrote of her childhood in Denver, Colorado. This lifelong love, combined with her instinctive need to rise to any challenge, helped her create the best-known American toy company in the world—Mattel—and the revolutionary fashion doll that became an international household word: Barbie.

The tenth child of Jewish immigrants from

Ruth Handler, four years old in this 1921 portrait, was the youngest of ten children.

Poland, Ruth Mosko was born in Denver, Colorado, on November 4, 1916. Her father, blacksmith Jacob Moskowicz, had landed on Ellis Island, the point of arrival for immigrants in the first half of the twentieth century, in 1907. Like many, he underwent an identity transformation on Ellis Island. Harried officials turned him into Jacob Mosko and put him on a train to Denver, where blacksmiths were much in demand for development of the Union Pacific Railroad.

Ruth's mother, Ida, stayed behind in Warsaw with their six children until enough money had been saved to bring them to America. In 1908 Ida, with the help of her oldest, twelve-year-old Sarah, brought the five younger children, Reuben, Lillian, Louise, Doris, and Max, on the arduous journey across the Atlantic Ocean, and the family was reunited in Denver. The last four children, Joe, Aaron, Maurice (known as Muzzy), and Ruth, were born in the family's new hometown.

Ida gave birth to Ruth at the age of forty. Sarah was twenty by then and newly married. When Ida needed surgery six months after Ruth's birth, Sarah took over the care of her infant sister, bringing her to the home she shared with her husband, Louie Greenwald. Ruthie never left. She grew up in Sarah and Louie's home, though she visited the rest of her family regularly. "The doors were never locked, and nobody had a key. They were always coming over," Aaron Mosko remembered. "We often had dinner together as a family." None of them found it strange that Ruthie lived with Sarah. "You see," he explained, "we had a large, ten-bedroom house, but it only had one bathroom. Sarah's home was nicer than ours, and it was just a few miles away." Sarah and Louie never had any children of their own, so Ruth lived the life of an only child in their home — but one with a loving brood of siblings nearby.

While love was strong between her and her parents ("I called them Ma and Pa," Ruth remembered, and she thought of them as "loving, indulgent grandparents"), communication was often difficult. Yiddish was the Mosko family language, and English was Ruth's. She spent much of her early childhood playing with Aaron and Muzzy.

Ruth's lively spirit is evident in this 1923 photo, taken when she was seven years old.

"The three of us were always together," Aaron recalled. "We were very close. Ruthie was the kind of kid who would do anything for anybody."

Ruth claimed that Sarah was "the greatest influence on the woman I was to become. She was a fantastic role model," Ruth wrote, "and I absolutely idolized her." "They were like mother and daughter," Elliot remembered. Although Sarah lacked any formal education, she had an acute business sense, and when Ruth was nine, Sarah and Louie bought a drugstore, which Sarah managed, across the street from Denver General Hospital. Like many drugstores in those days, it was not only a pharmacy but also a soda fountain, where people came for soft drinks as well as ice cream, coffee, and sandwiches.

Being a good "mother" as well, Sarah often gave Ruth dolls, trying, but always failing, to entice her little sister into traditional childhood play. By the time Ruth was ten years old, she chose instead to work at the drugstore after school, waiting on customers, attending the cash register, and being what was known as the "soda jerk"—the one who served sodas from the fountain, in the days before soda came in individual cans. She relished the job, even into her teenage years, favoring it over sleepovers and other activities with girlfriends.

For her sixteenth birthday, Ruth received a 1932 Ford convertible from Sarah and Louie. Trying the car out on a cruise downtown, Ruth first laid eyes on the boy who would become her lifelong partner in love and in work: Isidore Elliot

Handler. It was his head of black curls that first drew her attention and caused her to immediately decide he was "gorgeous." For his part, Elliot (then known as Izzy) claimed to have fallen in love with Ruth from a picture he saw in her parents' house when he came to visit her older brother Muzzy. Secretly attracted to each other from a distance, it wasn't long before they met at a dance and fell in love. "I asked her to dance," Elliot recalled, "and we danced like we'd been dancing together a long time. We melded."

Izzy was determined to become an artist, and Ruth's ambition was to become a lawyer. Her family, especially Sarah, was horrified at the thought of Ruth marrying a penniless artist and did everything possible to keep the two apart. Ruth and Izzy went along with her family's wishes, and each dated other people. "We listened to our parents," Elliot said. "But they couldn't separate us." Neither ever felt the same spark with anyone else as they did with each other, and in between other dates, they continued to meet.

Enrolled at Denver University, Ruth decided "on a lark," as brother Aaron described it, to take a summer trip to California with a girlfriend. Nineteen years old, she arrived in Hollywood. It was 1936, the heyday of the movie studios. Lunching with a friend who worked at Paramount Studios, Ruth made conversation by inquiring how one went about getting a job at a major movie studio. Her friend responded that it was impossible because everyone wanted to work in such glamorous surroundings. Ruth's passion to meet a challenge, which would define her life, arose. Within the day, she had a job at Paramount typing movie scripts. Back in Denver, Sarah was thrilled that Ruth had put a thousand miles between herself and the unpromising Izzy.

She had underestimated Izzy. He followed Ruth out to California and got a job as a lighting designer. For a year the two worked during the day and dated by night until Sarah, again taking matters into her own hands, fetched Ruth home to a secure future in Denver, where she could work for her lawyer brother Joe.

Living through another cold Colorado winter, away from both Izzy and the excitement of Hollywood, Ruth was miserable—and so was Izzy. He returned to Colorado and the two were married on June 26, 1938, with the blessings of the Mosko family, who finally accepted that Ruth would never be happy without Izzy. The newly married couple, craving the excitement of life in Los Angeles, knew they would always be restless in Denver. Immediately after the wedding, they drove west in their new blue Chevrolet, a wedding gift from Ruth's family.

Ruth went back to work at Paramount, and her husband, whom she now persuaded to go by his middle name of Elliot, had kept his job as a lighting designer. He also took classes at the Art Center College of Design, where he became drawn to the challenges and opportunities of industrial design. His dreams of becoming an artist faded as he encountered a new material just coming into use: an acrylic plastic known as

Lucite or Plexiglas. No household items as yet used this new material, and Elliot's creative mind filled with the possibilities. He began sketching ashtrays, hand mirrors, trays, bowls— everything one might need for furnishing a home. Ruth was so impressed with his sketches that she encouraged him to buy the expensive equipment needed to create samples in their half of a shared garage. She believed she could sell his pieces.

It was the first of many business risks the Handlers would take at Ruth's insistence. Elliot quit his job and school to create beautiful objects combining Lucite, metal, and wood; Ruth supported them through her work at Paramount.

While Elliot was shy and quiet, Ruth had an outgoing and persuasive personality. Still, she had to call upon all her courage the day she first took a suitcase of Elliot's samples into an exclusive Hollywood shop called Zacho's, where she was sure they belonged. Making her first sale, she found she relished the challenge. As she wrote in *Dream Doll:* "Adrenaline surged through me whenever I walked into a store with samples and walked out with an order." Elliot's creativity and Ruth's salesmanship were an unbeatable combination, though they struggled to maintain enough money to produce the orders that kept coming in.

In May 1941 their first child, Barbara, was born, and Ruth, following the custom of the times, became a full-time mother. In March 1944 she gave birth to Ken. Within months of his birth, Ruth finally admitted to herself that she needed to be a businesswoman as much as a mother. While she wanted to be with her children, she also understood that, as she told a reporter in a 1959 *Los Angeles Times* interview, "If I had to stay home I would be the most dreadful, mixed-up, unhappy woman in the world." In characteristic Ruth fashion, she took on one of the biggest challenges any woman can face: to be wife, mother, and businesswoman at the same time. That year, 1944, Ruth and Elliot formed a new company with their old friend Harold "Matt" Matson, in which Matt produced picture frames from Elliot's designs. The company name was formed from a combination of the partners' names: Matt-El, or Mattel. (Today we wonder why Ruth, always an intrinsic part of the business, was never part of the official company name. In *Dream Doll,* she reminds her readers that it was a different era then: "It was my idea to start with picture frames and I brought in that first big order. But this was 1944, and just as a woman got her identity through her husband in her personal life—you were Mrs. John Smith, not Sally Smith—should it not be so in business?")

At first Mattel made only picture frames. But Elliot's creative spirit was restless, and among his new designs was a line of dollhouse furniture. Ruth persuaded him to design a few other toys, and by Christmas 1944, Mattel was in the toy business.

Mattel grew steadily under the direction of Ruth and Elliot. Elliot designed the toys and Ruth ran the ever-burgeoning business. Their first big hit was a plastic toy ukulele, the colorful Uke-A-Doodle, which cost $1.49 in 1947. They followed that up with the first plastic baby grand piano and an innovative music box that allowed the company to create a variety of music-making toys. Each new hit brought its own problems—sometimes even disasters. For the Handlers, every one of them was another lesson in the rules of the toy business. By 1951 Mattel had six hundred employees (representing a wide range of races and nationalities) and a sixty-thousand-square-foot factory near the Los Angeles airport.

The biggest, riskiest decision Ruth and Elliot made was in 1955, when they were invited to advertise on a new weekly television show, *The Mickey Mouse Club*, produced by Walt Disney. Before televisions were a common item in most homes, toy companies rarely advertised directly to children and parents, except for a short period just before Christmas. Weekly advertising was unheard of for a toy company and would be breathtakingly expensive. In fact, it would take every penny Mattel had at the time.

Ruth took a gamble, betting that if they put Mattel's toys in front of children all year long, those children would walk into a toy store and ask for a particular toy by name. Even more important, she hoped, children would ask for those toys throughout the year, not only at Christmas.

Like most toy companies during those decades, Mattel sold most of its toys in the month or two leading up to Christmas. After nerve-racking weeks of no response to the advertising, just after Thanksgiving, orders began to pour in. Better still, stores began to stock Mattel's toys year round, as children and parents asked for the playthings they saw regularly on television. Thanks to Ruth's gamble, the toy business was changed forever.

As Mattel grew, Ruth found help for her home life, too. Sister Sarah, with her husband, Louie, moved to Los Angeles and helped care for Barbara and Ken. Eventually Elliot's widowed mother, Frieda, also moved nearby and became part of the support team.

Barbara, however, was never to be completely satisfied with anything less than an "ordinary" full-time mother, like her friends had. Barbara's disapproval and unhappiness brought Ruth many sleepless nights as she lay awake wondering if she was doing the right thing by struggling to fulfill her three roles at once. She made a tradition of reserving Saturdays for Barbara.

Among Barbara's favorite toys were paper

Ruth and Elliot were successfully running Mattel at the time of this 1952 photo with their children, Ken and Barbara.

dolls, and mother and daughter spent many a Saturday afternoon picking out new sets. In the late 1940s and early 1950s, there were dozens and dozens of paper dolls to choose from: babies, toddlers, young girls, grown-ups, and celebrities. Barbara and her friends, however, liked to play only with the paper dolls that represented adult women.

On the occasions when she was at home, Ruth would stealthily observe ten-year-old Barbara and her friends creating imaginary worlds for their adult paper dolls, playing out the possibilities of their own futures. And it was from a moment of motherhood, not from an astute business plan, that the seed that sprouted into the most revolutionary fashion doll in the world was planted.

"One day," Ruth recalled in *Dream Doll*, "it hit me. Wouldn't it be great if we could take that play pattern and three-dimensionalize it so that little girls could do their dreaming and role-playing with real dolls and real clothes instead of the flimsy paper or cardboard ones?" She envisioned a small, long-legged, narrow-waisted doll with fine adult details like finger- and toenail polish, eyeliner and eyelashes.

Mattel, which prided itself on not producing the same toys other companies were already making, had been looking for a unique doll to create. With her play-inspired revelation, Ruth was sure she had found it. But when she brought the paper dolls to Elliot and the design team, describing the doll she wanted them to create, she was told it would be impossible to produce something so detailed at a reasonable price.

Her husband should have known better than to use the word *impossible* with Ruth. While she appeared to accept the argument, her fighting spirit rose again. She grew determined to find a way to produce the doll she knew girls like her daughter would embrace. She believed, too, that while the official stumbling block was the high cost of production, the true reason her idea had been turned down was the male designers' discomfort with the idea of creating a doll with breasts. Even Elliot told her, "Ruth, no mother would ever buy her daughter a doll with breasts!" But Ruth was a mother, too, wasn't she? She tried to revive her idea several times over the next five years as Mattel, like many other toy companies, began to produce more and more of its toys in Japan, where manufacturing costs were dramatically lower. Even though she was the boss, the designers always came up with a good reason to turn down the idea.

Then came the fateful summer of 1956, when the Handlers, by now owners of the third-largest toy company in the world, took a family vacation to Europe. Ruth and fifteen-year-old Barbara, shopping in the mountain town of Lucerne in Switzerland, found themselves mesmerized before a shop window. The display featured six dolls straight from Ruth's vision of five years earlier: eleven inches high and slender, with a distinctly female shape, each one wearing a different European ski outfit.

Though Barbara had long outgrown her paper dolls, she still enjoyed displaying dolls in her room, and Ruth offered to buy her daughter one of the dolls, which, they learned, was known as Lilli. Barbara, torn between the different outfits, couldn't decide which one she wanted, but when Ruth asked if it was possible to buy the outfits separately, the saleswoman disdainfully informed her that if she wanted two different outfits, she had to buy two dolls. A light went on in Ruth's head.

The light shone even brighter the next day in Vienna, where they happened upon the same display in another store. Told again that it was impossible to buy an outfit without a doll, Ruth and Barbara bought two more of the dolls. Ruth knew she had found a model for the doll she would now insist Mattel produce.

That Ruth would see the play doll of her vision in Lilli is a testament to her far-reaching imagination. For Lilli, in spite of being a doll, was no children's toy. She was a German novelty toy for adults, based on an adult cartoon that had appeared regularly since 1952 in a German daily newspaper called *Bild-Zeitung*. It proved so popular that by 1955 a hard-plastic doll based on the cartoon was produced by a German doll company. Lilli looked like a long-legged, large-breasted, slim fashion model, with a very adult, hard expression. Her hair was pulled back severely into a ponytail, her eyebrows were narrow and sharply arched, her heavily made-up eyes held a sidelong look, and her red mouth was shaped into a near pout. She almost looked evil. Her cartoon adventures revolved around her suggestive relationships with men, and she was a popular joke gift for German bachelors, many of whom placed her on the dashboards of their cars, like a mascot.

Home in Los Angeles, with the proof of her idea in hand, Ruth would no longer take no for an answer. She knew that if a German doll factory could produce such a doll, a Japanese factory could do it even more affordably. She sent her chief engineer, Jack Ryan, along with product designer Frank Nakamura, a fluent Japanese speaker, to Tokyo with Lilli and the charge to find a manufacturer who could create a softer, vinyl version of the doll. Ruth planned that they would sculpt a new head and body and design their own clothes and accessories.

For three years Ruth pushed her team, both in Los Angeles and in Japan, to surmount the many technical problems of producing a small vinyl doll with the shape and details she demanded. She and Elliot hired Charlotte Johnson, a dress designer and teacher of clothing design at the Chouinard Art School, to design the first line of clothing for the doll, which quickly became known as Barbie—in honor, of course, of the ten-year-old whose paper doll play had inspired Ruth. The clothing Charlotte designed under Ruth's supervision was both glamorous and ordinary. Ruth wanted little girls to be able to dress Barbie for anything their imagination might conjure up, from a beauty pageant or nightclub performance to a football game or babysitting job. "My whole philosophy of Barbie," Ruth said later, "was that through the doll, the little girl could be anything she wanted to be, and I was worried that if she were too glamorous, little girls wouldn't be able to identify with her." Ruth's philosophy has endured for more than forty years, as Barbie today continues to have outfits that range from cutting-edge evening wear to clothing for every profession imaginable to basic jeans and T-shirts.

When the moment finally came to introduce Barbie to the world, the Handlers did so at the American International Toy Fair in New York City in 1959. Since 1902 toy companies from around the world gather in New York every February to show toy store owners what new playthings will be available that year—and to try to collect as many orders as possible.

Ruth was ecstatic over the successful realization of her vision; she predicted that Barbie would be a huge hit.

What did the toy buyers see in the Mattel showroom in February 1959? A curvy, long-legged blonde (or brunette) dressed in a black-and-white-striped strapless bathing suit, high-heeled backless sandals on her tiny arched feet, with sunglasses, hoop earrings, and a swinging ponytail.

The first Barbie, introduced in 1959, came in a box bearing drawings of her elegantly accessorized ensembles and cost three dollars.

Her heavy makeup bore some resemblance to her ancestor, Lilli; her eyes were rimmed in dark blue eyeliner; her red lips were almost pouty; and her eyebrows had that familiar high arch. She cost three dollars and came in a box bearing drawings of her elegant accessorized ensembles. Mattel announced her in their catalog as "a shapely teenage Fashion Model. . . . Girls of all ages will thrill to the fascination of her miniature wardrobe of fine-fabric fashions: tiny zippers that really zip . . . coats with luxurious linings . . . jeweled earrings and necklaces . . . and every girl can be the star. There's never been a doll like Barbie."

There *hadn't* ever been a doll like Barbie, and the toy buyers weren't sure what to do with her. Some bravely put in orders for the doll, but many didn't and expressed their disapproval directly to Ruth, with the same words she had heard from her own team at Mattel years earlier. "No mother will buy her daughter a doll with breasts," they warned. Others went further, trying to tell Ruth girls only wanted baby dolls so they could pretend to be mothers. Ruth knew the arguments by heart and, having finally won the battle at Mattel, was demoralized to have to fight it all over again. Girls don't just want to pretend to be mothers, she reiterated tiredly, but with no less force, to the toy buyers, "they want to pretend to be bigger girls."

While the toy store buyers' reaction to Barbie was a tremendous disappointment to Ruth, the new doll was by no means a failure. Orders came in slowly at first, but once Barbie appeared in Mattel's television commercials, girls started begging for her. The toy stores were swamped with orders all year long, and Mattel could hardly keep the doll on store shelves. At long last, Ruth had the satisfaction of knowing that her instinct of what girls wanted had been right, and even more important, she had the reward of being able to give it to them.

Barbie changed quickly over the first few years: her makeup grew softer, her hairdos changed yearly, and she began to look more like a real teenage girl. Her wardrobe expanded rapidly. Designer Charlotte Johnson would attend fashion shows in Paris and New York, then return to Los Angeles and create exquisite miniature fashions that echoed the most fabulous clothing of the day: red velvet evening coats with hats and slinky black strapless gowns. But she also designed clothes girls could imagine wearing in their own life: a full-skirted sky blue corduroy jumper named Saturday Night Date, slim jeans with a red-and-white-checked blouse for Picnic Set, and a short baby-doll pajama set, Sweet Dreams, that came with a little alarm clock and a diary.

It wasn't long before Ruth knew she had to create the ultimate teenage girl's accessory: a boyfriend. She wrote in *Dream Doll* that girls began writing letters asking for a boyfriend for Barbie that first year. Male dolls had never been successful, and Ruth was nervous about producing one. But thinking back to daughter Barbara's paper doll play, she remembered how important male paper dolls had been to the games, so she forged ahead to design a boyfriend for Barbie.

A popular teenager like Barbie needs a boyfriend, so Mattel introduced Ken.

In 1961 Ken—named after the Handlers' son—joined Barbie. The reaction from toy store buyers was similar to what it had been two years earlier, when they first saw Barbie, but most of them had learned enough from that experience to order at least a few Kens. And while Ken was never quite as popular as Barbie, he was popular enough. After all, Barbie needed somebody to show off those clothes to!

In fact, Barbie needed a whole circle of friends and family. Because of her then-unusual size and proportion, there were no other dolls that she could really hang around with. So, in 1963, Ruth created a best friend for Barbie, the freckled and friendly looking Midge. While Midge was nowhere near as glamorous as Barbie, she could wear all of Barbie's clothes, and a boyfriend eventually came her way, too: Allan. Soon Barbie also had a little sister, Skipper, who naturally had to have a friend, Scooter. In 1966 her family grew even larger when Mattel introduced her twin baby brother and sister, Tutti and Todd, and finally a cousin, Francie.

In addition to the dolls, Ruth's team continued to build an entire universe for Barbie, with games, books, furniture, cars, houses, a malt shop, and a drive-in movie theater. As technology improved, the dolls' bodies were able to twist and turn; legs could bend. Eventually they could even say phrases.

While Barbie was a teenage girl, some of her clothes reflected careers and opportunities both young girls and teenagers might daydream about. She had a teaching outfit, an airline attendant's uniform, a nurse's uniform, and, a few years later, a doctor's uniform. Today, of course, her wardrobe has expanded to include just about anything a girl might imagine doing: an astronaut suit, a firefighter's uniform, and even an ensemble called Paleontologist Barbie. "Barbie has always represented the fact that a woman has choices," Ruth wrote in *Dream Doll*.

Less than a decade after Barbie's introduction, the doll and

Mattel created a multitude of accessories for Barbie, including this peach-colored Irwin Sportscar with a turquoise interior.

her family were household words in most countries of the world. She had outgrown even Ruth's original vision. Ruth continued to direct that universe from her high position as Mattel's co-leader while continuing to run the company, which was now a giant in both the toy and the business world. Usually the sole woman in a room full of top businessmen, Ruth was often hurt and disappointed by the way she was treated by her male peers. Still, there was no ignoring her success, and the honors and appointments poured in. In 1958 she was the first woman ever elected to the board of directors of the Toy Manufacturers Association and in 1960 became vice president. A few years later she became the first woman in the United States to be appointed to the Federal Reserve Board, the central bank of the United States charged with the mission of maintaining the stability of the country's financial system.

After years of struggling to build Mattel, in 1970 Ruth and Elliot faced a new kind of struggle: Ruth was diagnosed with breast cancer, and one breast—and a few years later, the other—was removed. But Ruth turned her battle with cancer into a new challenge. Failing to find replacement breasts that fit and felt real, she embarked with her usual zeal on a new mission: developing a line of artificial breasts for women whose own breasts had been removed. Working with a partner, prosthetist Peyton Massey, Ruth named her line Nearly Me and the company she formed, Ruthton. Finally Ruth was part of a company name.

In the midst of Ruth's fight with cancer, she and Elliot were

Barbie became an even bigger success than Ruth could have ever dreamed. By 2000 Mattel was issuing reproductions of its early dolls, which adult collectors snapped up, along with hundreds of new Barbie styles, every year.

shocked to learn of unsavory business practices that had been taking place at Mattel. In spite of their protestations of ignorance and innocence, as heads of the company they were charged with fraudulent business practices and forced, in the late 1970s, to leave the company. They were both heartbroken to abandon what they had spent their lives building.

Being able to turn her energy and attention to the development of Nearly Me helped Ruth heal from her cancer and her business devastation. As she told a reporter: "When I conceived Barbie, I believed it was important to a little girl's self-esteem to play with a doll that has breasts. Now I find it even more important to return that self-esteem to women who have lost theirs."

While she continued to live a rich and energetic life, Ruth never completely vanquished the cancer that had taken hold in her body. She died in April 2002.

The story of Mattel is really a love story. Ruth and Elliot Handler created a sixty-four-year partnership from which they built a family, a company, and a doll that changed the world of play forever. Who, whether they love or hate the queen of fashion dolls, can imagine a world without Barbie? She is the seemingly immortal child born of the Handlers' dedicated partnership and their complementary creative and entrepreneurial visions. In the endurance of Barbie, we see the embodiment of the stamina and spirit of Ruth Mosko Handler, the girl who thrived on work, the young adult who couldn't resist a challenge, and the woman who never gave up a struggle.

Today's Women and the Future of Dolls

The pioneering women dollmakers of the nineteenth and twentieth centuries made radical changes in the world of dolls and play. Martha Chase's simple cloth dolls of the 1890s and Ruth Handler's vision of Barbie are a world apart. It is hard to believe they were played with in the same century. Yet descendants of both of these visionary women's creations—simple soft-cloth baby dolls and curvy well-dressed fashion dolls—live on happily, side by side.

PLEASANT ROWLAND

Probably the most dramatic step in dollmaking in the late twentieth century was taken by educator Pleasant Rowland when she created The American

In 1987 Pleasant Rowland posed with three original American Girl dolls (from left): Kirsten, Samantha, and Molly.

Girls Collection in 1986. Born in Illinois in 1941, Pleasant first worked as an elementary school teacher. Frustration with the materials provided for teaching reading led the self-motivated young woman to develop her own. Filled with energy and new ideas and committed to education, Pleasant soon left the teaching profession altogether and eventually became the author of reading and language arts programs used widely throughout schools in the United States. She might have pursued her rewarding career in educational publishing for many years more were it not for the experience of trying to find a doll as a

Christmas gift for a niece in the winter of 1984. For a second time, frustration led to a creative brainstorm. Her dissatisfaction with educational teaching materials had prodded Pleasant into generating her own; now her dissatisfaction with the quality of dolls available inspired her again. But Pleasant knew she was neither a designer nor an artist; she was an educator. A recent trip to Colonial Williamsburg had piqued her interest in historical interpretation. Pleasant's creative mind put it all together to form a company—Pleasant Company—that would simultaneously educate and entertain young girls. The company's American Girls Collection was the first to combine dolls of high quality representing American girls of various historical eras with historical fiction books. Period costumes, accessories, and furniture sold through a captivating color catalog directly to girls, their mothers, and grandmothers, the collection was an immediate hit. Its overwhelming consistent success resulted in sales of more than $300 million annually by 1998, when Pleasant sold the company to Mattel. Under Mattel's ownership, The American Girls Collection has continued to grow. Copycat competitors have come and gone, but none has captured the imaginations of contemporary girls like the fruit of Pleasant Rowland's vision.

Always eager to pursue new challenges, Pleasant Rowland put the American Girls behind her once Pleasant Company was safely in the hands of Mattel. Having successfully "passed the baton," as she sees it, to new owners, she established the

Pleasant T. Rowland Foundation and devotes herself to supporting the work of organizations dedicated to the arts, education, and historic preservation.

Although owned by Mattel, Pleasant Company has maintained an independent existence, expanding the American Girls Collection. In 2002 the company debuted a new book-and-doll series, this time for older girls, and named it Girls of Many Lands. To create the teenage dolls that would appeal to older girls, the company turned to one of the most respected doll artists of today: Colorado-born Helen Kish.

HELEN KISH

Known primarily to adult collectors, Helen has been sculpting dolls since the late 1970s. When Pleasant Company invited her to submit her designs for consideration for Girls of Many Lands, Helen leapt at the opportunity. "As a person who loves books and believes so much in giving girls power through education, I wanted to be part of this endeavor more than I had wanted anything for a long time," she says.

Helen's belief in giving girls power through education comes from her own life experience, growing up as the second of eight children in Denver in the 1950s. "We were a big, pretty poor family," she recalls, "though I don't think we children really knew that." Helen's childhood was filled with tomboy play with her six brothers and doll play with her younger sister. "We used to play dolls and nurse together,

Helen Kish was seven years old when this photo was taken.

because in my family, in the fifties, that's all girls were allowed to do—become a nurse or a teacher or, preferably, a mother." Because Helen loved babies more than anything, her favorite part of childhood was tending to her new baby siblings—and playing with her Tiny Tears baby doll. The idea of being a mother suited her fine, but her artistic urges always yearned for expression—and often took the form of dolls and sculpture.

"I was about seven when I began making my own paper dolls and designing the clothes for them. Then, when I was eleven, I began making cloth dolls, too," Helen relates. "And because I grew up in Colorado, where we had snow from the beginning of November right through March, snow was my first modeling medium. I was raised as a Catholic, so when everyone was making snowmen, I was trying to model the Virgin Mary."

Her family saw no need for a girl to go to college, nor could they afford it. A wealthy cousin, however, who recognized her talent and quiet ambition, arranged for a scholarship to a small teacher's college in Illinois. Helen quickly saw teaching was not for her. Education, however, was, so she came home and enrolled at the University of Colorado in Boulder as an art student. Unfortunately it was the late sixties, and the technique classes Helen craved were not in vogue. Disappointed, she made a summer visit to her brother in New York City, where she fell in love with Hungarian-born Tamas Kish.

Helen and Tamas came back to Colorado and married. Helen got a job and, with Tamas's encouragement, attended night school at the Rocky Mountain School of Art. "I knew that if I was going to have to work, I wanted to somehow work in the graphic arts." Commercial art school provided some of what Helen was hungry for, but it wasn't long before she was craving a baby. In 1975 the first of her three children was born, and it was during his infancy that Helen started modeling dolls out of a polymer clay called polyform. At first it was just a way to fill the time when Tamas was working or attending night school himself. But an encounter with a woman who made porcelain reproductions of antique dolls led her to master porcelain dollmaking and to create her own originals out of this fragile medium.

Relatives and friends applauded and supported her early efforts, and soon Helen found her way to the world of doll collectors and, from there, doll artists. She discovered the United Federation of Doll Clubs (UFDC), and at one of the group's conventions in 1978, she learned of the prestigious National Institute of American Doll Artists (NIADA). NIADA artists had a display of their work at the UFDC convention, and Helen's eyes were opened to the vast artistic possibilities of the

Petite Penelope is a porcelain doll made by Helen Kish in the 1980s.

medium. Her greatest admiration was for the work of Martha Armstrong-Hand. "Her work was the hottest thing in that room. She had a baby doll that people were clamoring to see." Eventually Helen had a chance to meet and talk with Martha, "and from that point on, it was my goal to be a better doll artist and a better sculptor so that I could be a member of NIADA."

She worked relentlessly at her sculpting, while raising her three young children, and finally reached that goal in 1981. She soon gained the admiration of other artists and of commercial doll manufacturers, who began to reproduce her designs. Adult collectors found her realistic and appealing figures of children and women both classically beautiful and heartwarming. Serving as president of NIADA in the early

Today Helen Kish is a well-known doll artist whose work is collected by adults and young girls alike.

1990s, Helen has, in her turn, inspired and encouraged many beginning doll artists. In 1991 she and Tamas formed Kish & Company and began reproducing her designs—which had previously been made only in porcelain—in vinyl, which was much more affordable and durable. Most important for Helen, who for a

In 2003 Pleasant Company introduced the Girls of Many Lands collection of dolls and books; the dolls were sculpted by Helen Kish.

long time lamented not attaining a college degree, she has been able to study sculpture with the renowned sculptor Bruno Lucchesi and to grow as a sculptor at the same time as she has been creating her dolls.

Her girlhood love for dolls has made designing Pleasant Company's Girls of Many Lands especially rewarding. While many of Helen's dolls for collectors look like toys, these are the first ones actually made for girls, rather than adults. She recognizes that all her artistic and commercial struggles of the past twenty years have led her to this point. "Everything has culminated in coming together with Pleasant Company. It's a perfect fit."

Key to the development of Helen's sculpting style was the encouragement and support, in those early years, of NIADA artist Martha Armstrong-Hand. "She was always very kind but very helpful in everything that she said. And one of the very best things she ever said to me was, 'Don't study dolls. Study sculpture.'"

MARTHA ARMSTRONG-HAND

Helen's close attention to Martha's advice now plays a part in furthering Pleasant Rowland's vision of dolls helping to educate girls. And in a pleasing reversal of life journeys, Martha Armstrong-Hand herself, before becoming known for her artistry, played an enormous role in creating beautifully sculpted dolls for children to play with. German-born Martha

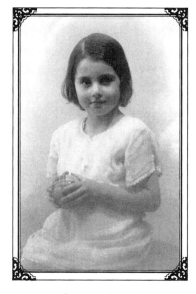

German-born Martha Armstrong-Hand spent her childhood in that country.

brought her training as an artist and sculptor to Mattel in the early 1960s. After creating such classic dolls as Pat-a-Burp, Cheerful Tearful, the Kiddles, and Buffy & Mrs. Beasley (to name just a few), she discovered the world of artist dolls in the mid-1970s. Now in her early eighties, she is revered among doll artists for her impeccably sculpted one-of-a-kind porcelain dolls and small editions. Her story is a bridge between the worlds of the earlier dollmakers and today's artists.

Born in 1920 in Berlin, Martha came of age during the country's political turmoil that preceded World War II. Her father was a teacher and her mother, who was much younger, had been one of his students. The difference in age did not make for a successful marriage, and Martha's mother left the family when Martha was quite young. Martha was raised by her father and, when he remarried, first by one stepmother then, after her death, by another, though she saw her mother frequently.

Martha remembers first modeling in clay at her Montessori

school when she was three. "I remember we were supposed to make a snake," she says. "Everybody rolled out some kind of noodle, but I made a real snake with a head and a pattern on the back." Her early childhood was plagued by illnesses, and she would occupy herself modeling in plasticine while in bed. Not only was she ill but throughout her later childhood both her stepmother and then her father were seriously ill. Living in a household that felt like a hospital, Martha kept herself busy with art and added puppet making to her repertoire before the age of eleven.

Her mother, Nita, was Jewish, and as the Nazi regime grew stronger in Germany in the 1930s, Nita escaped to England. Martha herself, being half Jewish, began to experience persecution by her schoolmates. Her beloved father died in 1936, which Martha, then sixteen, describes as a "shock." The pain of his death was helped by the growing closeness between her and her second stepmother, Hilde Sass, who Martha came to call Mutter Hilde (Mother Hilde).

Martha's formal art education began with a two-year apprenticeship with a wood-carving professor, and she grew quite skilled at wood carving. At the age of eighteen she enrolled at the Academy of Arts and chose sculpture as her specialty while taking courses in drawing, art history, and porcelain painting. "I loved every minute of it," Martha says, "and managed to ignore (tune out) what was going on in the world."

What was going on in the world was, of course, the start of World War II, and Martha's Jewish ancestry became more and more of a barrier to her art studies. In December 1944 the threat of a Russian invasion caused many Germans, including Martha and Mutter Hilde, to flee. "In January 1945, with two suitcases and the clothes on our backs, my widowed step-mother and I made an arduous six-hundred-mile journey by oxcart and train to a small farming community in northern Germany . . . where I carved grave crosses, furniture decorations, even a couple of primitive wooden dolls. When the British arrived, I worked as an interpreter and met my future husband, Sam Armstrong, an Irishman in the British Army."

In 1948 Martha and Sam married, and in 1949, with their three-month-old daughter, Jessie, they immigrated to the United States and settled on a ranch outside of Los Angeles. They raised chickens and had three more daughters. Meanwhile Martha tried to make money at something artistic: "from float design to cake decorating . . . I gave classes in papier-mâché, taught crafts at a summer camp, sculpted figures for View-Master, made puppets for Bob Baker's Marionette Theater and created special effects for George Pal Productions." Then came the fateful day in 1960 when a graphic arts agency sent her to Mattel, where Elliot and Ruth Handler, flush with the success of their newest doll, Barbie, were looking for somebody to model a head for a doll that would be called Chatty Cathy. When the child pulled a string in the back of

Chatty Cathy, the doll would speak. Martha's head sculpture was used for Chatty Cathy, but she was not hired by Mattel until 1963 and then it was as a face painter.

Martha was burning to be one of the company's sculptors. She finally got the position when a "burp" sound that had been created demanded a new sculpture. "Now the burp needed a baby," Martha recalls in her unpublished memoirs. "The Handlers had left instructions to model some infant head while they were traveling abroad and the whole sculpture department was busy with wrinkled babies. When the Handlers returned, they didn't like a single one. New babies were

Martha Armstrong-Hand is surrounded by some of the many dolls she designed for Mattel in the 1960s and 1970s.

born . . . and to my delight I was asked to contribute to the frantic effort. All the doll heads were wigged and set on temporary bodies, and all the women in the department voted. I was told that Ruth Handler picked up my Number 13 and hugged her. I was a sculptor at Mattel!"

The doll that kicked off Martha's sculpting career at Mattel was called Pat-a-Burp. In the years that followed, Martha sculpted and collaborated on dozens of dolls at Mattel, including many of Barbie's friends. Her sculpting studies, her puppetry, and her earlier work making animation models for View-Master (a company that makes three-dimensional slides to be watched through a viewer) all came together in the work she thrived on at Mattel until 1975, when she decided to consult for the company from her new home in the small coastal village of Cambria in California.

Satisfying as her collaborations at Mattel had been, "I knew I wanted to be the sole creator, from the original idea to the last tiny stitch in the hem," Martha says.

Her need to work on her own dolls came after she saw an exhibit of NIADA dolls in Los Angeles. "Each artist showed creations that were theirs from start to finish and I felt as if I had entered a new world," Martha writes in her book *Learning to Be a Doll Artist*. "I started to dream, and I can't count the images that lived in my head at that time." She began to sculpt Melissa, a sturdy little porcelain toddler with highly realistic features. It took her four years to complete her first original

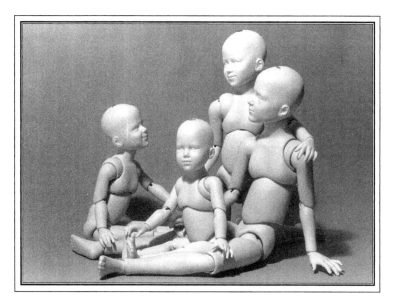

This photo of the unclothed porcelain dolls created by Martha Armstrong-Hand in the 1980s reveals their remarkable body sculpting as well as the many joints that make them so posable.

doll, but she found the many years of sculpting play dolls for Mattel a perfect foundation for the sculpting of her own original porcelain children. She eventually became renowned among doll artists for her anatomically perfect children's and babies' bodies and faces.

Death had taken Sam Armstrong from her in 1967 and divorce had separated her from her second husband, Bob Sherman, in 1972. In 1976 she met David Hand, a director at Walt Disney studios, who had directed films such as *Snow White* and *Bambi*. They married six months later. Martha credits David with instilling in her the commitment to pursue her own dollmaking. "He became my manager and my slave driver," she says with a laugh. She lived happily with David in Cambria until his death in 1986.

Known by fellow artists as a meticulous sculptor and a generous and inspiring teacher, Martha continues to sculpt and teach in Cambria, traveling occasionally to conferences and artist gatherings. Her work has already been deeply influential both in the toy industry and in the development of doll artistry. Yet when people remark on her talent, she deflects the compliment by saying, simply: "I've been practicing for more than fifty years." That urge for practicing is rooted in her deep conviction that: "Re-creating the essence of life in three-dimensional form is still my reason for living."

ROBIN WOODS

Like Martha Armstrong-Hand, doll designer and entrepreneur Robin Woods has furthered the work begun by women such as Martha Chase and Beatrice Alexander. Like Pleasant Rowland, Robin is an educator who did not enter the doll business until she had enjoyed a successful career in a different field. And like Helen Kish, as a girl Robin loved dolls. In spite of these similarities to her peers, however, Robin Woods has a singular story that reaches back into the traditional toy industry and ahead to the future of play dolls.

Robin was born in Lubbock, Texas, in 1943 and spent much of her childhood living there with her grandparents, in a big

On her seventh birthday, Robin Woods (at right) and her best friend showed off their dolls, which wear clothes made by Robin for her birthday party.

house a few blocks from the campus of Texas Tech University, which had been founded by her great-grandfather. Her mother's youngest siblings were still living at home, and for Robin they were like her own siblings. When her mother remarried and moved to Santa Fe, New Mexico, Robin spent school years with her mother and summers with her grandmother. Her childhood was marked by doll play with friends, alone, and, most important, she claims, with her grandmother.

"She was my best friend, she was my playmate, she had a fabulous imagination, and she could tell stories like no one I had ever known. . . . She had a degree in home economics and she was a trained pattern maker, and we would make clothes for all the dolls in the house every summer," Robin explains. Her eventual career was certainly foreshadowed by the long summer afternoons playing with her grandmother. "We would play doll factory," she continues. "We would set up all the dolls and decide to make two dresses for each of the dolls. Then we would pick out the fabric and make the patterns and make them all at once."

In spite of such focused childhood play, Robin, like many girls of that era, was not encouraged to think about careers. Her family hopes centered on her being married, and as for a career—she was told that a woman could be a teacher or a nurse. She rebelled against both options.

"In fact, I used to say that when I grew up, I was going to have a doll factory," she says. "And I had no idea what that meant! But as I roller-skated around town, I would pretend that the sidewalks were made of glass and I could look down and see clothes being sewn and coming down the production line. And actually, when I did start my own doll factory, I drew on those memories for trying to figure out how to do it."

There were many years and a multitude of experiences between roller-skating through Lubbock and the creation of Robin Woods, Inc., in Pittsburgh in 1983. Robin earned bachelor's and master's degrees in literature, married a musician, moved to Pennsylvania, worked with child welfare agencies, adopted two children through the agencies, divorced, moved to Pittsburgh, remarried, started a nursery school, and earned a PhD in child development. And all that occurred by 1976.

In 1976, already mother of five children (the two she had adopted plus two adopted and one biological child of her second husband's), Robin gave birth to their daughter Mimi. But it was her studies in child development that turned her attention back to dolls. "What I found most intriguing was the power of toys and the importance of play. Having grown up in a childhood where I had all the time to play that I wanted and tremendous support for a wonderful play life, with plenty of time for fantasy and pretend and loving literature and learning about characters, I realized that my children had never had any of that."

That realization was just a tiny seed, but it had been planted. Robin worked as a mental health coordinator for a health maintenance organization and found herself terribly depressed by the dramatic loss of jobs that resulted from the end of Pittsburgh's steel industry. She knew that the only help most of her clients needed was a job. "I had been playing around with the idea of starting a doll business," she says, and now she decided to take the idea seriously. She found aid and advice through the American Women's Economic Development and other organizations dedicated to helping women start businesses. She wrote a business plan, found a factory, secured a loan from the Small Business Association and additional money from a wealthy friend, and in 1983 Robin Woods, Inc., opened up shop. Twelve workers produced cloth dolls of Robin's design, meant for children's play. Wearing elaborate clothing and boasting hand-painted eyes, the dolls were created in series with names like Camelot Collection

In 1993, while working for the Alexander Doll Company, Robin Woods designed a special doll with a wardrobe set called Alice Visits the Gardens of Disney.

and Poetry of Childhood, reflecting Robin's love of literature and costuming.

With the opening of her factory, Robin achieved both her childhood fantasy of owning a doll factory and her adult ambition to offer jobs to Pittsburgh's unemployed. Her company did well. In 1987 she brought in some big investors, and her company grew even more rapidly. By 1990 she had 450 employees and a well-established name and reputation in the doll world. But, she recalls, "the greed factor of the people who had invested so much money began to take the company under." In 1991 she was forced out of the company that still bore her name.

By now Robin's style of design and the high quality of her costuming were so well known that the new owners of the Alexander Doll Company, who had bought the company just three years earlier from Madame Alexander herself, hired her. The new owners believed that the company had become too focused on creating dolls for adult collectors and that Robin could bring them back into the play doll business. She started a collection called, aptly, Let's Play Dolls, which bore her look of beautifully designed clothing with layers of wonderful fabrics and sweet faces with hand-painted eyes. By 1994, though,

Robin Woods visited with young girls at a doll shop in 1993; they hold two of her dolls.

the Alexander Doll Company was on the brink of bankruptcy. "They just didn't have the money to do what they planned, and wanted, to do," Robin explains. She was jobless again.

Once more she was snapped up—this time by the oldest doll company in the United States, Horsman, where she was named director of design and development, creating new collections of dolls for children and for collectors. It was a time of upheaval in the doll industry, with many new companies starting up business and many old and venerated ones struggling to hold on. Horsman was among the latter, and after two years there, Robin found herself looking for work.

With her reputation, work was never hard to find. Everybody believed a Robin Woods design could save their company. She became a freelance designer, working for such companies as Kingstate, Effanbee, and The Family Company. Wherever Robin went, her dolls were nominated for awards, and every company she worked for won at least one award for a Robin Woods doll.

Her second marriage had broken up, and her daughter Mimi, her youngest child, was an adult by now, so Robin moved herself to Colorado Springs and pursued another ambition: designing theatrical costumes. Several fulfilling years followed, but the lure of doll design never left her alone. She moved back to Texas in 1999, married a childhood sweetheart, and started a new doll company: Robin Woods Country. Having learned her lesson, she is keeping her output small and

When Robin Woods decided she wanted to create a doll collection with a story about the digital world, she came up with the Digigirls, which were introduced in 2001.

under her own control. And she continues to design dolls for other companies when she is presented with a good idea. One of her favorite projects was the creation of six Digigirls for Toys "R" Us in 2001. "The idea was to create a doll line that had a story about the digital world," explains Robin. "The Digigirls go to a school where every kid has a laptop computer and they're online all the time with kids all over the world. They discover an evil entity running around cyberspace who wants to steal children's imaginations in order to get an imagination himself." The vinyl dolls are fourteen inches high and have funky and interesting clothes, which, Robin says, were influenced by a lot of different cultures. "Each one came with a digibank, in which they could keep their e-mail addresses and other information," Robin adds.

In spite of their trendiness, the Digigirls were not the success Toys "R" Us and Robin hoped for—"the timing was just terrible, coming after 9/11," she concedes. But she still believes the story of the Digigirls is a good one for today and hopes to produce them again soon. "I want every doll to tell a story; a doll without a story has no meaning." A girl who grew up loving dolls more than anything, Robin's purpose has always been straightforward: "I have always wanted to make the most beautiful doll possible for a child."

Yue-Sai Kan

Still, not every child loves dolls the way Robin Woods did. Dolls were not a big part of Yue-Sai Kan's childhood. Born in Guilin, China, but raised in Hong Kong in the 1950s as the daughter of a widely respected painter, Yue-Sai had a sophisticated cultural upbringing. The oldest of four girls, she was not particularly interested in toys. In fact, she recalls, "I used to disembody toys the moment I got one. I was too curious." She does remember having a tricycle, which she rode at her family's country home, along with pursuing many outdoor activities. "I climbed trees and mountains and fought with boys!"

As a little girl in China, Yue-Sai Kan was too much of a tomboy to be very interested in dolls.

Her parents were very strict and didn't hesitate to inflict physical punishment, a practice Yue-Sai still believes is a good way to learn right from wrong. At the same time they were very supportive of her constant wishes to learn new things, be it dance, music, or French. She began ballet and piano lessons at the age of four, and music soon became a serious focus of her life. While she loved school, she describes herself as a "mediocre student," more interested in participating in glee club and drama club than in academics. Her ambition, however, was to be a pianist.

She took a major step toward fulfilling this ambition by winning a scholarship to Brigham Young University in Hawaii to study music. "I loved being in school in Hawaii," she says. "People were so special there; there was no racial tension at all and people were very loving and generous." It was while she was at Brigham Young that her interest in different cultures was sparked. "Because I was in a multiracial school, I learned a great deal about many cultures, especially Asian and Polynesian ones," she notes.

Yue-Sai earned a degree in music, but after years of practicing eight hours a day, she made a heart-wrenching decision. "I felt that I could never be another Rubenstein. And if you can't be the best at something, why do it?" She gave up her childhood ambition.

In 1972, giving in to a longtime desire, she moved to New York City. "I felt lost when I got here; it is such a sophisticated and scary city—so European, compared to Hawaii, which had been very Asian." With her sister Vickie, she began an import-export trading business with China. At the same time, she volunteered to host a cable television show in New York that broadcast in both English and Chinese. Having experienced firsthand the gap in understanding between Asia and the West, she soon realized that television was a powerful means of bridging that gap. Her passion grew to promote a connection between Asia and the West, and in 1978, through her own production company, Yue-Sai Kan Productions, she started a weekly series called *Looking East*. The series, which stayed on the air for twelve years, introduced Eastern cultures and customs to America. Yue-Sai's dynamic personality, as well as the depth of the programs, brought the series awards and critical acclaim. Yue-Sai became well known as the first television journalist to connect the East and West, and she went on to make numerous other documentaries about Asia for broadcast in the United States, including the Emmy Award–winning *China — Walls and Bridges* for ABC.

Dividing her time between New York City and Shanghai, Yue-Sai developed a personal awareness of what Asian women lacked that American and European women had. Frustrated with the difficulty of finding makeup for her skin tones and Asian features, she founded a cosmetics company for Asian women in 1992 with the aim of "enhancing those qualities that are singularly Asian, so Asian women can realize how beautiful they really are." It seems only natural that after focusing on Asian women's needs, she would turn her attention to Asian girls and the great lack of authentic Asian play dolls. In 1999, she says, "I discovered that all over China, there was no doll with black hair and black eyes." Once she decided to fill this need, she had to learn a whole new business—as she had done with television production and then with the cosmetics industry. "I had to learn how to make a doll from scratch, as well as proper management." The dolls were introduced in China in 2000 and in the United States in 2001. Yue-Sai says she is "still learning" the doll and toy business, but the Yue-Sai

Panda Protector Wa Wa is one of the vinyl Asian fashion dolls produced by Yue-Sai Kan's company Yue-Sai Wa Wa.

Wa Wa doll collection (*wawa* means "doll" in Chinese) already has more than sixty different styles and can be found in stores like FAO Schwarz and Toys "R" Us. The dolls are vinyl fashion dolls with Asian hair and features. They have shiny black hair, almond-shaped eyes, and Asian skin tones, and their wardrobes include contemporary and traditional clothing—Chinese wedding gowns along with khaki pants and turtlenecks. Some of the dolls are dressed as professionals: one popular model is a pediatrician. Most are made and priced for children's play, but there are a few limited editions for collectors as well.

For Yue-Sai, who has also written three books, funded scholarships for students in both China and the United States, and won numerous entrepreneurial awards, dolls are just one important part of her larger aspiration. "I want to be the one to have introduced the world to China and to have made the Chinese people's lives more beautiful," she says. "It is my hope that the brand name Yue-Sai will last beyond me." The little girl who wanted to learn everything loves her life today. "I feel accomplished and I feel loved," Yue-Sai reflects happily.

LORNA MILLER SANDS

Often it takes time to find your creative path. For Lorna Miller Sands, as for many of the women in this book, the wait was well worth the result. Born in Nassau, in the Bahamas, in 1963, Lorna always knew she would become well known for "something." She didn't discover that something—dolls—until she was in her late twenties. The fifth of seven children, Lorna was raised by her mother and grandmother and led a happy, busy life, playing with her younger brother and sister, swimming in the Carib-bean, drawing, and singing for her moth-er's friends to the accompaniment of her older brother's guitar. Her mother, whom Lorna de-scribes as a "go-getter," worked in the hotel industry

In this circa-1975 photo, Lorna Miller Sands and her younger sister are dressed for a festive evening in the Bahamas, where the artist was born and spent her childhood.

and was one of the first women in the Bahamas to manage, and later own, a resort. "She taught me that nothing in life is handed to you; you have to work for everything you want," Lorna recalls.

Lorna was a smart girl who skipped the third and fourth grades and was always drawing. Her talent was admired by children and adults alike. "One of my teachers in elementary school was so impressed by a picture of mine that she gave it to the principal, and the principal framed it and put it up in her office." When it came time for college, Lorna applied to art schools in the United States and, at the age of sixteen, enrolled at the California College of Arts and Crafts in Oakland, California. Influenced by the healthy work ethic of her mother, Lorna majored in graphic design. "It was the practical thing to do. It isn't practical to just get a degree in drawing!" Love of art soon overcame practicality, however, and when she graduated in 1984, it was with a degree in drawing. Ever realistic, she took a job working for a telemarketing company and painting the occasional portrait. "I was just biding my time," she admits. "I got married and I had two little boys. The bills had to be paid."

She bided her time until 1990, when, during a visit to a friend in Hamburg, Germany, she saw some artist-made dolls. Their beauty immediately impelled her to action. "It was the lightbulb thing," she says. "I realized, 'I can do that!' I just knew I had the ability and background to create my own

Lorna Miller Sands's
black baby dolls like
Xander, which is about
twenty inches long, are
prized for their realistic
appearance.

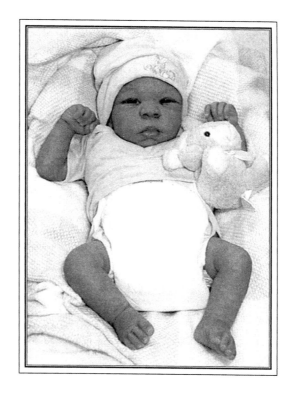

dolls." She came home to El Sobrante, California, "unpacked my suitcase, and went and got some clay." She began to sculpt immediately, and although she didn't think much of her early efforts (she had never sculpted before), her fellow workers loved her work. Just eight months after attempting her first sculpture, she sold several dolls at a small California doll show in the Bay Area. In spite of the heady experience of selling her work, Lorna says, "Let's get realistic! I wasn't going to quit my job and sculpt dolls full-time."

The immediate success of her work, she believes, has a lot

to do with her subject: black children. While black dolls have been made for centuries, Lorna's work stood out for its realism. "People kept saying they'd never seen anything like this before." Her twenty-one- to twenty-four-inch dolls represented mischievous, naughty, stubborn, or gleeful young children, complete with chubby cheeks, liquid eyes, sparkling teeth, and sometimes tongues. An article about her in *Dolls* magazine in early 1994 seemed to capture the essence of her work with its title: "Everyday Kids with Attitude."

By 1992, with a few awards and steady sales under her belt, Lorna was finally confident enough to leave her job and devote herself to dollmaking. She enjoyed her great success with dolls, but in 1995 she had another baby, and "that changes your priorities," she notes. She slowed down her dollmaking, eventually stopping altogether. But by 2001 she couldn't stay away from her art and began making dolls again, this time devoting herself to black babies. "Whoa, did I find myself or what?" she exclaims when she talks about her discovery of baby dolls. "I'd been sculpting dolls for eleven years, and when I started doing these babies, I knew the reason I was put on this planet." At nineteen to twenty-two inches in size, her baby dolls can wear infant clothing right off the rack, which is a pleasure for Lorna. Clothing her dolls had always been her least favorite part.

A fourth baby of her own was born in 2002, but Lorna has managed to keep making dolls while tending to her family. She works at home, and her husband, who works part-time, helps

Today Lorna Miller Sands is the
mother of four children and countless
hand-sculpted baby dolls.

with her business. Until recently, her dolls have been
one-of-a-kind creations or
very small editions, which
means the dolls are so expensive that only adult col-
lectors can buy them. "I have always wanted to have more of
my dolls out there," she notes, and recently the Middleton Doll
Company, which is known for its vinyl dolls of high quality,
has reproduced the first of Lorna's black babies in vinyl. While
not quite a child's play doll, it is a step in that direction, for the
Middleton Doll Company also produces fine vinyl play dolls.

It is a necessary step, for Lorna is unique in being a black
artist creating authentic black baby dolls with the potential for
being played with. Just as Yue-Sai Kan filled a need in creating Asian dolls for Asian children, so could Lorna fill a large
hole in the world of play dolls. But for her, where her dolls end
up is not the important thing. "I put my heart and soul into
these babies," she says. "I've been very blessed—that I can
make these creations and that people want to buy them. But
even if I never sold any of them, I would have the same happiness in making them. It's about the happiness."

As Lorna has learned, happiness is not the goal; it is part of the journey. Many paths, dotted not only with happiness, but also with struggle and frustration, lead to dolls. There are often detours and backtracking along the way. Still, all the women in this book have found creative and personal satisfaction in that journey. Their legacies live on in the work of those who succeed them, and in the hearts of the children whose lives have been enriched by their creations.

Dolls are playthings, and as we grow, many of us leave our playthings behind. Yet some of us never lose our love for dolls. As we mature, we appreciate them for many things: the fantasies they inspired, the comfort they provided—or perhaps for the beauty of their clothing or the efficiency of their construction. But how many of us ever think about the person whose imagination gave life to a beloved plaything? How many girls ever consider directing their creative instincts into dolls?

As the women in this book learned, there is no reason to abandon dolls when we leave childhood. Your love for dolls may inspire you to study and collect, or you may find it leads you to a worthy artistic and commercial pursuit. As each dollmaker builds on the work of those before her, dolls continue to evolve. Perhaps you will be the next pioneer. Dollmaking opens a world of new possibilities to those who enter it, a world in which sweet memories of childhood mingle with new frontiers of creativity, power, and mature fulfillment. For what could be more rewarding than to turn your work into play?

Resources

You can learn more about dolls and dollmakers by visiting museums, reading magazines and books, or joining a club or an organization. The following list, while by no means exhaustive, will help you get started.

Don't forget to check local newspapers for doll shows and sales. These are not just for buyers; attending is a good way to educate yourself. Most dealers and artists are happy to share information with interested, polite newcomers to the doll world.

ORGANIZATIONS

United Federation of Doll Clubs (UFDC)
10900 North Pomona Avenue
Kansas City, MO 64153
816-891-7040
www.ufdc.org
Founded in 1949, this umbrella organization is made up of doll clubs around the country and the world. UFDC also has a Junior Collector program for those under eighteen years old.

The organization hosts regular conventions, has a library and museum in its headquarters, publishes its own magazine, and rents slide programs on a multitude of subjects relating to dolls.

National Institute of American Doll Artists (NIADA)
www.niada.org
Dedicated to the art of the doll, this artist organization also has a strong patron membership of collectors and others interested in contemporary doll creations. Quarterly newsletters are published, and a yearly conference is held. Conference attendance, as well as the exhibition of members' work, is always open to the public.

Original Doll Artists Council of America (ODACA)
www.odaca.org
This artist organization also includes a strong membership of collectors and enthusiasts and holds an annual one-day luncheon and exhibition.

**National Antique Doll Dealers'
Association (NADDA)**
www.nadda.org
A society of antique doll dealers,
NADDA holds several doll sales a
year around the country. Whether or
not you are prepared to buy, visiting a
sale is a great opportunity to learn
about antique dolls.

SPECIALTY CLUBS
AND WEB SITES

Friends of Sasha
PO Box 187
Keuka Park, NY 14478

Madame Alexander Doll Club
PO Box 330
Mundelein, IL 60060–0330
847-949-9200
www.madc.org

Modern Doll Collectors, Inc.
www.moderndollcollectors.com

www.barbiecollectibles.com

www.sashadolls.com

MAGAZINES

Antique Doll Collector
6 Woodside Avenue, Suite 300
Northport, NY 11768
631-261-4100
www.antiquedollcollector.com

Barbie Bazaar
5711 8th Avenue
Kenosha, WI 53140
262-658-1004
www.barbiebazaar.com

Contemporary Doll Collector
Scott Publications
30595 Eight Mile Road
Livonia, MI 48152
800-458-8237
www.scottpublications.com

Doll Crafter
Jones Publishing
PO Box 5000
Iola, WI 54945
800-331-0038
www.jonespublishing.com

Doll Reader
44 Front Street, Suite 590
Worcester, MA 01608
800-437-5828
www.dollreader.com

Dolls
Jones Publishing
PO Box 5000
Iola, WI 54945
800-331-0038
www.dollsmagazine.com

GENERAL WEB SITES

www.dollshow.com
www.virtualdolls.com
www.collectdoll.about.com
www.dollymaker.com

DOLL MUSEUMS

There are many doll museums of varying size and quality around the country and around the world. Those listed below are some of the ones with more substantial collections in the United States. The only museum outside the United States that appears in this list is one in Switzerland that is devoted to the work of Sasha Morgenthaler.

Puppenmuseum Sasha Morgenthaler
Museum Bärengasse
20–22 Bärengassestrasse
Zurich, Switzerland

Yesteryears Doll Museum
Main and River Streets
Sandwich, MA 02563
508-888-1711

Wenham Museum
132 Main Street
Wenham, MA 01984
978-469-2377
www.wenhammuseum.org

The Doll Museum
980 East Main Road
Portsmouth, RI 02871
401-682-2266
www.dollmuseum.com

Shelburne Museum
U.S. Route 7
PO Box 10
Shelburne, VT 05482
802-985-3346
www.shelburnemuseum.org

Museum of the City of New York
1220 Fifth Avenue at 103rd Street
New York, NY 10029
212-534-1672
www.mcny.org

Strong Museum
1 Manhattan Square
Rochester, NY 14607
585-263-2700
www.strongmuseum.org

Philadelphia Doll Museum
2253 North Broad Street
Philadelphia, PA 19132
215-787-0220
www.philadollmuseum.com

Mary Merritt Doll Museum
843 Ben Franklin Highway
Douglassville, PA 19518
610-385-3809
www.merritts.com/dollmuseum
    /default.asp

Washington Dolls' House and Toy
    Museum
5236 44th Street NW
Washington, D.C. 20015
202-363-6400
www.dollshousemuseum.com

Angela Peterson Doll & Miniature
  Museum
101 West Green Drive
High Point, NC 27260
336-885-3655

Johnny Gruelle Raggedy Ann and
  Andy Museum
PO Box 183
110 East Main Street
Arcola, IL 61910
217-268-4908
www.raggedyann-museum.org

Toy and Miniature Museum
  of Kansas City
5253 Oak Street
Kansas City, MO 64112
816-333-2055
www.umkc.edu/tmm

The Eugene Field House and
  St. Louis Toy Museum
634 South Broadway
St. Louis, MO 63102
314-421-4689
www.eugenefieldhouse.org

Denver Museum of Miniatures,
  Dolls and Toys
1880 Gaylord Street
Denver, CO 80206
303-322-1053
www.coloradokids.com/miniatures

Enchanted World Doll Museum
615 North Main
Mitchell, SD 57301
605-996-9896
www.cornpalace.org/dollmuseum

McCurdy Historical Doll Museum
246 North 100 East
Provo, UT 84606
801-377-9935
www.utahvalley.org/visguide
  /ATTRACTS/Mccurdy.htm

Land of Enchantment Doll Museum
5201 Constitution NE
Albuquerque, NM 87110
505-255-8555

Rosalie Whyel Museum of Doll Art
1116 108th Ave. NE
Bellevue, WA 98004-4321
425-455-1116
www.dollart.com

Bibliography

BOOKS

Armstrong-Hand, Martha. *Learning to Be a Doll Artist*. Livonia, MI: Scott Publications, 1999.

Beard, Lina and Adelia B. *The American Girls Handy Book: How to Amuse Yourself and Others*. New York: Charles Scribner's Sons, 1887, 1888. Reprint Lincoln, MA: David R. Godine Publishers, 1987.

Biffiger, Stefan, ed. *Sasha-Puppen/Sasha Dolls*. Wabern-Berne, Switzerland: Benteli Verlag AG, 1999.

BillyBoy. *Barbie: Her Life and Times*. New York: Crown Publishers, 1987.

Coleman, Dorothy S., Elizabeth A., and Evelyn J. *The Collector's Encyclopedia of Dolls*, vol. 2. New York: Crown Publishers, 1986.

Finnegan, Stephanie. *Madame Alexander Dolls: An American Legend*. New York: Portfolio Press, 1999.

Formanek-Brunell, Miriam. *Made to Play House: Dolls and the Commercialization of American Girlhood, 1830–1930*. Baltimore, MD: Johns Hopkins University Press, 1998.

Goddu, Krystyna Poray, ed. *The Art of the Doll: Contemporary Work of the National Institute of American Doll Artists*. N.p.: National Institute of American Doll Artists, 1992.

———— and Wendy Lavitt. *The Doll by Contemporary Artists*. New York: Abbeville Press, 1995.

Handler, Ruth, with Jacqueline Shannon. *Dream Doll: The Ruth Handler Story*. Stamford, CT: Longmeadow Press, 1994.

Johl, Janet Pagter. *The Fascinating Story of Dolls*. Watkins Glen, NY: Century House, 1941, 1970.

King, Constance. *The Collector's History of Dolls*. New York: St. Martin's Press, 1978; Bonanza Books, 1981.

Kruse, Käthe. *Das Grosse Puppenspiel: Mein Leben*. Duisburg, Germany: Verlag Puppen & Spielzeug, 1951, 1992, 1996.

Lavitt, Wendy. *American Folk Dolls*. New York: Alfred A. Knopf, 1982.

Lord, M. G. *Forever Barbie: The Unauthorized Story of a Real Doll*. New York: William Morrow and Company, 1994.

Osborn, Dorisanne. *Sasha Dolls Through the Years*. Annapolis, MD: Gold Horse Publishing, 1999.

Reinelt, Sabine. *Käthe Kruse: Die frühen Jahre/The Early Years*. Duisburg, Germany: Verlag Puppen & Spielzeug, 1994.

———. *Käthe Kruse: Auf dem Höhepunkt ihres Schaffens/At Her Creative Peak*. Duisburg, Germany: Verlag Puppen & Spielzeug, 2000.

Richter, Lydia. *The Beloved Käthe-Kruse-Dolls: Yesterday and Today*. Cumberland, MD: Hobby House Press, 1983, 1991.

Wilder, Laura Ingalls. *Little House in the Big Woods*. New York: HarperCollins Publishers, 1932, 1971.

ARTICLES

Bischoff, Karen. "A Legend Among Her Peers: Martha Armstrong-Hand." *Dolls* (January/February 1989): 38–42.

Calvert, Catherine. "Madame Alexander: Dolls and Dreams." *Town & Country* (December 1983): 46–64.

Edward, Linda. "'To Protect Our Children': The Story of the Chase Stockinette Doll." *Antique Doll Collector* (October 2001): 35–40.

Fecher, Louise. "Everyday Kids with Attitude." *Dolls* (January 1994): 58–61.

Goddu, Krystyna Poray. "Madame Alexander: The Woman Behind the Name." *Dolls* (November 1988): 58–62.

Kershaw, Sarah. "Ruth Handler, Whose Barbie Gave Dolls Curves, Dies at 85." *New York Times* (April 29, 2002).

Lovaas, Kati. "The Dolls of Käthe Kruse, Yesterday and Today." *Dolls* (April 1991): 58–66.

———. "The Dolls of Käthe Kruse, Yesterday and Today, Part 2." *Dolls* (May 1991): 67–73.

Noble, John Darcy. "Plain and Fancy Handiwork." *Dolls* (October 1990): 71–75.

Nolan, Helen. "An American Master of Cloth." *Dolls* (February 1995): 74–77.

Van Maanen, James. "The Dolls That Helped to Save a City." *Dolls* (December 1988): 40–44.

Votaw, Anne and Anne Barden. "Sashas—the First Generation." *Dolls* (January 1991): 64–72.

Ward, Cynthia. "Unmistakably Madame." *Private Clubs* (November/December 1986): 22–26.

Whitton, Margaret. "Martha Jenks Chase, Turn of the Century American Doll Manufacturer." *Doll Reader* (October 1984): 94–99.

Witt, Kathy. "Babies on the Brain." *Dolls* (April 2002): 60–63.

BROCHURES AND CATALOGS

Alexander Doll Company Catalog Reprints: 1942–1962, vol. 1. Brockton, MA: Barbara Jo McKeon, n.d.

Doggart, Sara. *Where Do Sashas Come From?* Stockport, England: Trendon Ltd. Brochure, 1982.

Formanek-Brunell, Miriam. *Dolls and Duty: Martha Chase and the Progressive Agenda*. Providence, RI: The Rhode Island Historical Society, 1989.

Sasha Morgenthaler Doll Museum brochure, Zurich, Switzerland, 1988.

UNPUBLISHED MEMOIRS AND DIARIES

Armstrong-Hand, Martha. Unpublished autobiography, n.d.

Chase, Martha. Personal journal, October 1876–July 1878, unpublished manuscript, archives of the Strong Museum, Rochester, NY.

WEB SITES

Fortune. "How We Got Started: Pleasant Rowland" (http://www.fortune.com/ fortune/fsb/specials/innovators/rowland.html).

Hansen, Chris. "Insight: America's Highest Paid Woman." The Home Based Business Council, Inc. (http://www.medusaonline.com/hbbc/insight_ 009.htm).

Yue-Sai Kan Web site (http://www.yue-saikan.com/english/eg_index.html).

Acknowledgments

I am grateful to the many people who played a role in bringing this book to life. I thank those who helped me obtain interviews, photographs, and other research materials, especially Dorothy McGonagle of Skinner Auctions, Carol Sandler of the Strong Museum, Linda Edward, Nancy Smith, Miriam Formanek-Brunell, Kristen Hammerstrom of the Rhode Island Historical Society, Andrea Christensen and Marion Hohmann of Käthe Kruse Puppen GmbH, Laura Knusli, Dorisanne Osborn, Lynton Gardiner, Jane Abrahams of the Alexander Doll Company, Elliot Handler, Aaron Mosko, Mark Harris of McMasters Harris Auction Co., Marti Sebree, Pleasant Rowland, Michelle Watkins, and Kathleen Saal for her translation work.

Thanks to Martha Armstrong-Hand, Helen Kish, Robin Woods, Lorna Miller Sands, and Yue-Sai Kan for granting me lengthy interviews and loaning photographs.

I am always keenly aware, and appreciative, of the many researchers and writers who came before me and whose work informs my own, especially the splendid and singular late John Darcy Noble.

I want to thank my editor Christy Ottaviano for her enthusiastic belief in this book and for her intelligent direction and

Yona Zeldis McDonough for steering me toward Christy. I am grateful to Amy Belk, Lucy Kummerlee, Annie Quick, and Jack Scaparro for being the first to listen to these stories; to Kathryn Black for her enduring friendship, guidance, and inspiration; to Tom Farrell for his loving support and steadfast partnership; and to Anna Goddu and Jack Goddu for their boundless patience and, especially, for sharing the excitement.

Photo Credits

Every effort has been made to contact the owners and photographers of the photos used in this book. I regret that not all could be located and therefore that some of these images may not be credited in full. The publisher will be pleased to make the necessary arrangements at the first opportunity.

Jacket Photos
Front flap: Courtesy Nancy Smith; front panel, back panel (top left): Courtesy Alexander Doll Company; back panel (bottom left): Courtesy Yue-Sai Kan; back panel (bottom right): Courtesy Elliot Handler

Martha Chase
11: Private collection/Reproduced from *Dolls and Duty: Martha Chase and the Progressive Agenda, 1889–1925*, published in 1989 by the Rhode Island Historical Society; 14, 17: Courtesy Nancy Smith; 20: Courtesy the Museum Doll Shop; 22: Private collection

Käthe Kruse
31: Courtesy Käthe Kruse GmbH; 33: Private collection/Photo by Lynton Gardiner; 36, 37, 38, 39: Courtesy Käthe Kruse GmbH

Sasha Morgenthaler
41, 42: Copyright © Community of heirs of Sasha Morgenthaler; 48, 49, 50, 51, 52, 53: Private collection/Photos by Dorisanne Osborn

Beatrice Alexander Behrman
56: Courtesy William and Kathleen Blotney Birnbaum/Photo by Lynton Gardiner; 66: Courtesy Portfolio Press/Photo by Walter Pfeiffer; 71, 72, 73, 75, 76: Courtesy Alexander Doll Company

Ruth Handler
78, 79, 86: Courtesy Elliot Handler; 91, 94, 95: Courtesy McMasters Harris Auctions Inc.; 97: Courtesy Elliot Handler

Today's Women and the Future of Dolls
100: Courtesy Pleasant Rowland; 103, 105, 106 (top and bottom): Courtesy
Helen Kish; 108, 111, 113: Courtesy Martha Armstrong-Hand; 115, 118, 119,
121: Courtesy Robin Woods; 123, 125, 126: Courtesy Yue-Sai Kan; 127, 129,
131: Courtesy Lorna Miller Sands